Thomas Carew, Arthur Vincent

**The Poems**

Thomas Carew, Arthur Vincent

**The Poems**

ISBN/EAN: 9783744710800

Printed in Europe, USA, Canada, Australia, Japan

Cover: Foto ©Thomas Meinert / pixelio.de

More available books at **www.hansebooks.com**

# THE POEMS

## OF

# THOMAS CAREW

*Thomas Carew*

# THE POEMS
## OF
# THOMAS CAREW

### EDITED BY
### ARTHUR VINCENT

LONDON:
LAWRENCE & BULLEN, Ltd.
16 HENRIETTA STREET, W.C.
1899.

NEW YORK:
CHARLES SCRIBNER'S SONS,
153-7 FIFTH AVENUE.
1899.

*Richard Clay & Sons, Limited,
London & Bungay.*

# CONTENTS.

|  | PAGE |
|---|---|
| INTRODUCTION | xiii |
| Bibliographical Note | xxxvii |

POEMS—

| | |
|---|---|
| The Spring | 1 |
| To A. L. Persuasions to Love | 2 |
| Lips and Eyes | 5 |
| A Divine Mistress | 6 |
| A Beautiful Mistress | 7 |
| A Cruel Mistress | 8 |
| Murdering Beauty | 9 |
| My Mistress commanding me to return her Letters | 10 |
| Secrecy Protested | 13 |
| A Prayer to the Wind | 14 |
| Mediocrity in Love Rejected | 16 |
| Good Counsel to a Young Maid | 17 |
| To my Mistress sitting by a River's side | 18 |
| Conquest by Flight | 19 |

## CONTENTS.

|  | PAGE |
|---|---|
| POEMS— | |
| To my Inconstant Mistress | 20 |
| Persuasions to Enjoy | 21 |
| A Deposition from Love | 22 |
| Ingrateful Beauty Threatened | 23 |
| Disdain Returned | 24 |
| A Looking-glass | 25 |
| An Elegy on the La: Pen: | 26 |
| To my Mistress in Absence | 29 |
| To Her in Absence | 30 |
| Eternity of Love Protested | 31 |
| Upon some Alterations in my Mistress, after my Departure into France | 32 |
| Good Counsel to a Young Maid | 33 |
| Celia Bleeding | 34 |
| To T. H., a Lady resembling my Mistress | 35 |
| To Saxham | 36 |
| Upon a Ribbon | 39 |
| To the King, at his Entrance into Saxham, by Master John Crofts | 40 |
| Upon the Sickness of E. S. | 42 |
| A New-Year's Sacrifice | 44 |
| To one who, when I praised my Mistress' Beauty, said I was blind | 45 |
| To my Mistress, I burning in Love | 46 |
| To her again, she burning in a Fever | 47 |
| Upon the King's Sickness | 48 |
| To a Lady, not yet enjoyed by her Husband | 50 |
| The willing Prisoner to his Mistress | 51 |
| A Fly that flew into my Mistress' Eye | 52 |

## CONTENTS.

|  | PAGE |
|---|---|
| Celia Singing | 53, 54 |
| To one that desired to know my Mistress | 55 |
| In the Person of a Lady to her Inconstant Servant | 56 |
| Truce in Love Intreated | 57 |
| To my Rival | 58 |
| Boldness in Love | 59 |
| A Pastoral Dialogue | 60 |
| Grief Engrossed | 63 |
| A Pastoral Dialogue | 64 |
| Red and White Roses | 66 |
| To my Cousin (C. R.) Marrying my Lady (A.) | 67 |
| A Lover, upon an Accident necessitating his Departure, consults with Reason | 68 |
| Parting, Celia Weeps | 69 |
| A Rapture | 70 |
| Epitaphs on the Lady Mary Villiers | 76 |
| Epitaph on the Lady S. | 78 |
| Maria Wentworth | 79 |
| On the Duke of Buckingham | 80 |

FOUR SONGS BY WAY OF CHORUS TO A PLAY—

| The First of Jealousy | 83 |
|---|---|
| Feminine Honour | 85 |
| Separation of Lovers | 86 |
| Incommunicability of Love | 87 |

SONGS IN THE PLAY—

| A Lover, in the Disguise of an Amazon, is dearly beloved of his Mistress | 88 |
|---|---|
| A Lady, Rescued from Death by a Knight | 89 |

## CONTENTS.

PAGE

POEMS—

| | |
|---|---|
| To Ben Jonson | 90 |
| An Hymeneal Dialogue | 92 |
| Obsequies to the Lady Anne Hay | 94 |
| To the Countess of Anglesey | 97 |
| An Elegy upon the Death of Dr. Donne, Dean of Paul's | 100 |
| In Answer of an Elegiacal Letter, upon the Death of the King of Sweden from Aurelian Townsend, inviting me to write on that Subject | 104 |
| Upon Master W. Montague, his Return from Travel | 108 |
| To Master W. Montague | 109 |
| On the Marriage of T. K. and C. C. | 111 |
| For a Picture, where a Queen Laments over the Tomb of a slain Knight | 112 |
| To a Lady, that desired I would Love her | 113 |
| Upon my Lord Chief Justice | 115 |
| To A. D., Unreasonable, distrustful of her own Beauty | 117 |
| To my Friend G. N., from Wrest | 120 |
| A New-Year's Gift. To the King | 124 |
| To the Queen | 125 |
| To the New-Year, For the Countess of Carlisle | 126 |
| To my honoured Friend, Master Thomas May, upon his Comedy, The Heir | 128 |
| To my worthy Friend, Master George Sandys, on his Translation of the Psalms | 129 |

## CONTENTS.

|  | PAGE |
|---|---|
| To my much honoured Friend, Henry, Lord Carey of Leppington, upon his Translation of Malvezzi | 131 |
| To my worthy Friend, Master Davenant, upon his excellent Play, The Just Italian | 132 |
| To the Reader of Master William Davenant's Play | 133 |
| To my Friend, Will. Davenant | 135 |
| The Comparison | 136 |
| The Complement | 137 |
| On Sight of a Gentlewoman's Face in the Water | 140 |
| A Song | 141 |
| The Second Rapture | 142 |
| The Tinder | 143 |
| A Song | 144 |
| The Carver | 146 |
| To the Painter | 147 |
| Love's Courtship | 149 |
| On a Damask Rose | 150 |
| The Protestation | 151 |
| The Tooth-ache cured by a Kiss | 152 |
| To his Jealous Mistress | 153 |
| The Dart | 154 |
| The Mistake | 155 |
| On Mistress N. | 156 |
| Upon a Mole in Celia's Bosom | 157 |
| An Hymeneal Song, on the Nuptials of the Lady Ann Wentworth and the Lord Lovelace | 158 |

## CONTENTS.

PAGE

POEMS—

| | |
|---|---|
| A Married Woman | 160 |
| A Divine Love | 161 |
| Love's Force | 163 |
| A Fancy | 164 |
| To his Mistress | 165 |
| In Praise of his Mistress | 166 |
| To Celia, upon Love's Ubiquity | 168 |
| To Mistress Katherine Neville, on her Green Sickness | 170 |
| Mr. Carew to his Friend | 171 |
| To his Mistress retiring in Affection | 172 |
| On his Mistress going to Sea | 174 |
| Methodus Amandi | 175 |

APPENDIX TO POEMS—

| | |
|---|---|
| The Hue and Cry | 179, 180, 181 |
| Song | 182 |
| To his Mistress Confined | 183 |
| The Guiltless Inconstant | 185 |

CAREW'S MASQUE—

| | |
|---|---|
| Coelum Britannicum | 191 |
| First Song | 224 |
| Second Song | 227 |
| Third Song | 230 |
| Fourth Song | 232 |

NOTES ... 237
LIST OF FIRST LINES ... 261

# INTRODUCTION.

THE biographer of Thomas Carew is foredoomed to execute but a shadowy work. He lacks the material to present a living picture, and is compelled by the seriousness of his task to restrain the desire to draw on the imagination for what is missing. Thomas Carew must have been something more than the writer of the poems which bear his name, but if it was his wish that all else of him should be effaced, he had it so far as any one, not an utter nonentity, could hope or expect. With greater regard for the curiosity of posterity, his father, Sir Matthew Carew, Master in Chancery, drafted an autobiographical note to be cut in the stone of his monument in St. Dunstan's-in-the-West. In due time the stone was made to set forth that Sir Matthew was Cornish by birth, Doctor of Laws, and *Miles* by blood; that he was the tenth child of the family of nineteen which his father, Sir Wymond Carew, had by his wife, Martha, sister of Anthony Denny; that he married Alice Ingpenny, widow of Sir John Rivers, Lord Mayor of London, and that of their many children only three, Matthew, Thomas, and Martha, survived their father, who died, aged seventy-six, August 2, 1618. The exact number of Sir Matthew's children is not to be certainly ascertained, but the names of eleven of them have come down, and it is an instance of the unkindness of fate that, although the church registers of St. Dunstan's and of West Wickham in Kent are eloquent of more than any one has yet desired to know about Elizabeth, Alice, Francis, Audrey, Wymond, Hyman, Walter, and William Carew, both they and other records are silent as to Thomas.

Of Martha, the eldest child of Sir Matthew and the pride of his old age, we know that she made two good marriages, and of Matthew, the elder surviving son, that he was knighted at the age of nineteen for bravery in the Irish wars; that he settled at Middle Littleton, Worcestershire, and that in his marriage with his sister's stepdaughter he maintained the family tradition of philoprogenitiveness.

It is to the registers of Oxford University we owe the knowledge that Thomas Carew was born in 1594 or 1595, for it there appears that when he matriculated as a member of Merton College, June 10, 1608, he was thirteen years old, and had been born in Kent. After having been admitted to the B.A. degree, January 31, 1611, he was entered at the Middle Temple. His progress in legal studies was not such as to satisfy his father, who in a letter written February 25, 1613, to Sir Dudley Carleton complained that one of his sons was roving after hounds and hawks, while the other was studying in

the Middle Temple, but doing little at law. Sir
Dudley had married Anne Savile, a niece of Sir
Matthew, and had thus earned the privilege of
receiving in confidence the tale of all the woes
that beset his wife's uncle. Most of the old lawyer's
troubles were due to heavy losses caused by specula-
tion in land and by over-great trust in friends, as
he put it, and the recital of them was not seldom
accompanied by a request for the favour of a loan.
But the rising diplomatist was also expected to find
remedies for family failings, and, as Thomas Carew
was clearly not suited for the law, he was sent to join
Sir Dudley's household at Florence, Carleton being
English ambassador at Venice. His stay could not
have been long, as Carleton returned some time in
1613, but on being appointed ambassador at the
Hague in 1616 he agreed to keep Thomas Carew
with him as secretary.

In April 1616, Sir Matthew is writing to Sir
Dudley, hoping his son Thomas will do well. Less
than five months later he is writing again, regretting
the precipitate return of Thomas, who had been sent
home by his employer with a recommendation to the
service of Lord Carew. The real cause of Thomas
Carew's dismissal was the discovery by Carleton that
his secretary had been slandering or making insinua-
tions against himself and his wife. Whether from a
wish to spare the father's feelings, or not to damage
the young man's career, Carleton sent him away with-
out disclosing the true reason, but at the same time
he appears to have written an account of the facts to

his correspondent and gossip, Edward Sherburn, who effectually put a spoke in young Carew's wheel whenever he was in a fair way of getting employment. Carew, who, not knowing that he had been found out, seems to have imagined that the introduction to Lord Carew given him by Carleton was the outcome of a desire for his advancement, is found very shortly after his return home writing to Carleton a long account of his ill-success with Lord Carew. This letter, which is one of three written by Carew that have been preserved, is a long one, and two extracts are, perhaps, enough to serve as a fair example of the writer's epistolary style:

"Right Honourable, my most singular good Lord,—

"I have been thus long in giving your Lordship account of the success of my business, by reason of my Lord Carew's absence from this town, where after I was arrived, and had a while consulted with my father and other friends, it was thought fit I should repair unto him to the Queen's Court; which then, with the King and Princes, was at Woodstock, where I delivered your Lordship's letter. His answer to me was, that he had already in that employment a Master of Arts, whose seven years' service had not yet deserved to be so displaced; and added, that I, being his kinsman, might expect from him all those greatest courtesies whatsoever, whereunto his nearness of blood did oblige him, which I should always find him ready to perform; but to admit me into his family as a servant, it were a thing (said he) far beneath your quality, and which my blood could not suffer without much reluctance."

After repeating the arguments with which he had

failed to move Lord Carew, and expressing the opinion that he was not likely to get anything from him but fair words and compliments, Carew proceeds to enlarge on his chances with Lord Arundel, another possible patron suggested by Carleton. In the event of another refusal he innocently anticipates being able to return to Carleton's service,

"from which, I profess (notwithstanding all these fair shows of preferment), as I did with much unwillingness depart, so do I not without great affliction discontinue; my thoughts of their proper and regular motion not aspiring higher than the orb of your Lordship's service; this irregular [motion] being caused by your self, who are my *Primum mobile;* for I ever accounted it honour enough for me to *Correre la fortuna del mio Signior,* nor did I ever aim at greater happiness than to be held, as I will always rest,

"Your Lordship's most humble devoted to your service,

THO. CAREW."

"*London,* this 2 of *September,* 1616."

Carew was equally unsuccessful with Lord Arundel as with Lord Carew, for after promising to give him the appointment if he could shake off two competitors, Lord Arundel, who had heard of the incident at the Hague, fobbed him off. Sherburn advised the rejected candidate to try his fortune with the rising favourite, Viscount Villiers, but Carew had, as he wrote in another letter to Carleton, no appetite to hazard a third repulse, and retired to his father's house in Chancery Lane.

*b*

If Carew had hopes of paternal commiseration he chose an unfortunate time, for Sir Matthew was just then losing £12,000 "through one whom he trusted," and had, moreover, got to hear of the real reason for his son's return to England. He was very angry, as Sherburn, who was probably the informer, reported to Carleton, and ordered his son to write a letter of submission. Thomas would seem to have defended himself and to have refused to write any apology, preferring to wander idly without employment, according to his father's account, though not more than six weeks had passed since the young man's homecoming. The weeks, however, went by, and two months later, Thomas was, on the same authority, leading a vagrant and debauched life. He failed to find any regular occupation, and a year after his return Sir Matthew is still found pleading to Carleton, for the sake of their relationship and ancient friendship, to pardon his son Thomas. Whatever the precise nature of the offence may have been, it required much purging, and Lady Carleton was little disposed to forgiveness. She returned to England in March 1618, and her uncle, afraid apparently to meet her, wrote humbly hoping the misconduct of his son would not diminish their natural affection, and assuring her he would have turned him off had he not been repentant. In the following August Sir Matthew died, and there is an end of his querulous letters and an end also of the only portion of Thomas Carew's history which exists in any fulness.

In his life and his death, the old Master in Chancery

was his son's worst enemy. He put no sort of faith
in him, and looked upon him as a source of trouble
only; he did not live to see his son outgrow youthful
indiscretion and develop a very exceptional talent,
and he left behind him, among Carleton's corre-
spondence, a series of letters which treat of, but do
not fully unfold, what was, so far as is known, the one
discreditable episode in the young poet's career. And
this single episode of boyhood is practically all that
remains of Carew outside of his work. The story of
the rest of his life has to be pieced together from
casual references, and the blanks cover far greater
periods of time than the facts. His character has
to be judged not from what he did, but, in the
manner approved by the proverb-maker, from his
acquaintances.

Freed from his father's help or hindrance, Carew
was not long in obtaining a situation, and he was one
of the hundred and odd persons who formed the train
of Lord Herbert of Cherbury when he started from
Dover in March 1619 as ambassador to France.
Among Herbert's other "principal gentlemen" were
John Crofts, a life-long friend of the poet's, and
Edmund Taverner, the musician. Herbert's auto-
biography is silent as to the doings of his train
except when he himself was also directly concerned,
and Carew comes in for no further special mention.
It may be assumed that he accompanied Herbert in
his several journeys about France, and it is certain
that a part of his leisure was employed in the com-
position of verses to the mistress he had found for his

heart before he left England. No clue has ever been found as to the identity of this lady; nothing can be inferred from the name Celia, which was a generic name for the loves of seventeenth-century poets, and even if the person so addressed by Carew was always the same, there is little information about her to be gleaned from the poems she inspired. These, however, convey the impression that there was some real person hidden under the name, although they have little to say as to any particular attributes which might lead to her identification. She was not beautiful, if we may trust the judgment of one who, when the poet praised his mistress's beauty, said he was blind (p. 45), but, if the poet himself may be trusted, she had a soul-stirring voice (pp. 53, 54); she could weep when her lover left her (p. 69); but, when he came back from France, he noticed some alterations (p. 32); perhaps she had begun to alter when she commanded the return of her letters (p. 10), and, to judge from the general tone of what may be taken to be subsequent addresses to her, she was never the same again.

When this damaging absence of Carew in France came to an end has not been certainly determined. Lord Herbert of Cherbury was temporarily recalled in July 1621, and his ambassadorial duties were brought to a final end in April 1624. For anything that is known to the contrary, Carew may have stayed till the latter date, and have returned to attach himself to the Court, which "he followed before he was of it." Herbert's further influence, if any, on Carew's career is not traceable, for it does not appear that he did anything for him except to allude to "my witty Carew" in a gratulatory poem prefixed to a volume of verse. That Carew made himself agreeable to the Court is to be inferred from the fact that in 1628 he received the appointment of gentleman of the privy-chamber, and a year or two later that of sewer [1] to the king. But with this meagre list of the honours he won, the record of facts which can be stated with any degree of certainty about Thomas Carew comes to an end. Anything else is but the gossip of story-tellers or such guesswork as may result from speculating on Carew's own poems or those of others. The glimpses of his life to be thus obtained show that if not particularly distinguished, it was in part, at least, a merry one.

It is to "old G. Clarke, Esq.," formerly Lord of the Admiralty and Secretary to Prince George of Denmark, who related the anecdote to Sir John Percival, that we owe a pleasing insight into royal life at Whitehall and Carew's courtly manners. According to this authority, Thomas Carew, gentleman of the privy-chamber, was going to light King Charles into the queen's chamber, when he saw Jermyn, Lord St. Albans, with his arm round her neck; he stumbled and put out the light. Jermyn escaped: Carew never told the king, and the king never knew it: the queen heaped favours on Carew. Tom

---

[1] *Sewer* was the officer at court whose duty it was to taste of the dishes intended for the royal table, to serve them and to remove them.

Killigrew sketches another scene at Court in which he was disputing with the lady he afterwards married, Cecilia Crofts, one of the queen's maids-of-honour, and Carew was called in to arbitrate, and requested to write a song on Jealousy (p. 83). The jealousy is to be presumed to have been the private affair of the lovers, and not to have concerned the poet personally, for, in the absence of any kind of evidence beyond the similarity of name, the temptation to connect Cecilia Crofts with the Celia of the poems must be resisted. Cecilia was a beauty and a favourite at Court, and Carew was an intimate friend of her brother John, who was also attached to the king's service, and through him of the numerous family of Crofts. He stayed at their seat at Saxham in Suffolk, where he seems to have been uncommonly pleased with the handsome treatment he received (p. 36), and he was invited again to act as domestic poet on the occasion of a royal visit. His inscription on the tomb of Cecilia's niece, Maria Wentworth (p. 79), is among the best known if least deserving of his compositions.

But although Cecilia Crofts was claimed by another and "Celia" was fickle and disdainful, Carew did not languish without love of some sort or another. In Suckling's correspondence is a "letter to a friend to dissuade him from marrying a widow which he formerly had been in love with and quitted." Suckling's friend was apparently Thomas Carew, whose reply, or supposed reply to the letter was printed with it in parallel columns, paragraph for paragraph. Neither composition is very savoury. The argument of

Suckling was directed against all marriage, and more particularly against marriage with a widow, "a kind of chewed meat": the answer extolled marriage, and the writer says, "I will marry, and . . . I'll marry a widow . . . 'tis princelike to marry a widow for 'tis to have a taster." But Suckling's correspondent may have been the same "T.C." to whom a verse-letter was addressed on the same subject by Fletcher, the translator of Martial, who can hardly have been Carew: in any case it is scarcely possible that the lady numbered so many years as specified in the lines,

> If thou wilt needs to sea, oh, must it be
> In an old galiasse of sixty-three?

It seems certain that the project if ever formed was never carried out, and Carew continued to be unfortunate in love. How great was his misfortune is shown by some verses of Suckling written on the occasion of Carew being afflicted with the result of an unhappy selection of an object for his love, and his continued illness from the same cause is alluded to in another letter of Suckling's.

The easy terms of familiar friendship existing between Carew and Suckling are perhaps only typical of the good fellowship which bound Carew and a large number of acquaintances all more or less well known. With Jonson, Selden, Cotton, John Vaughan, Sir Kenelm Digby, and Thomas May he was included among "the chief acquaintance" of Lord Clarendon while that grandfather of queens was a student at law, and "stood at gaze and irresolute what course of life to take," and was described by him as "a person of pleasant and facetious wit." His own poetical addresses to friends extend Clarendon's list with the names of Aurelian Townsend, George Sandys, Lord Carey of Leppington, Davenant, Walter Montague, and Donne, who as incumbent of St. Dunstan's-in-the-West was for a time Carew's parish priest, and who exercised a notable influence on his writings. John Hales, of Eton, who was chaplain to Sir Dudley Carleton while Carew was secretary, and who had a special charge of the poet's soul, was of the number, which further included Robert Baron, who in his *Pocula Castalia* addresses "Dearest Tom, Love's Oracle," Shirley, who borrowed, or anticipated the same phrase ("Carew . . . must be no more the oracle of Love,") Clement Barksdale, the author of *Nympha Libethris*, who sent to Carew, while he was staying with John Crofts, an early copy of Davenant's poems with some Latin verses of his own, Henry Lawes, who found music for many of the poet's songs, and James Howell. The letters of the last-named have fortunately preserved an anecdote in which Carew figures. Under date April 5, 1636, Howell wrote to Sir Thomas Hawk :

"I was invited yesternight to a solemn supper by B. J., where you were deeply remembered ; there was good company, excellent cheer, choice wines, and jovial welcome: one thing intervened, which almost spoiled the relish of the rest, that B. began to engross all the discourse, to vapour extremely of himself and by vilifying others to magnify his own Muse. T. Ca.

buzzed me in the ear, that though Ben had barrelled up a great deal of knowledge, yet it seems he had not read the *Ethics*, which, among other Precepts of Morality, forbid Self-commendation."

The B. J. of this letter is plainly Ben Jonson, and T. Ca. is Thomas Carew, who at the age of forty could afford to speak slightingly of the man who had doubtless extended a helping hand to him in his youth, as he did to many another promising poet who was "sealed of the tribe of Ben." Jonson, indeed, had found him serious work as his assistant in the historical research required for his history of Henry V., one of the works which, while lying in the author's desk, fell victims to Vulcan's appetite; for it is difficult to see, despite the epithet "noble," to what other Carew the reference can be in the lines

> And in story there
> Of our fifth Henry, eight of his nine year,
> Wherein was oil, besides the succours spent,
> Which noble Carew, Cotton, Selden lent.

But Carew, though he could admire Jonson, was alive to his failings, and there is a flavour of patronage about some of his lines to "dear Ben," written when the older man was sore from the failure of his play (p. 90). Nothing from Carew's pen was included in *Jonsonus Virbius*, the collection of elegies written in honour of the great man after his death, though from the line

> Let Digby, Carew, Killigrew, and Maine,

in Falkland's contribution to the volume it would seem that something was expected of him. Illness or written or, at any rate, were not prefixed to the edition of 1636. And in that same year the marriage of Anne Wentworth with Lord Lovelace, which took place July 9, 1638, was celebrated by Carew with a hymeneal ode (p. 158). This negative evidence is supported by the positive history of another man who has been confounded with Thomas Carew. The history is that of Thomas Carey, and when it is remembered that in the seventeenth century the name Carew was habitually, as sometimes now, pronounced Carey, it is fortunate that even greater confusion has not been made between Thomas Carew and Thomas Carey.

Thomas Carey was the second son of Robert Carey, Earl of Monmouth, and was born at Berwick-on-Tweed, being baptized there Sept. 16, 1597. Like Carew, he went to Oxford, but his college was Exeter and his matriculation and degree-taking each three years later. He, too, was attached to the Court and was made a great favourite by James I., acting as his secretary, and receiving the appointment of groom of the bed-chamber. Among the manuscripts at the British Museum is a vellum-bound volume in Carey's own handwriting containing "all the king's short poems that are not printed." In his character of confidential secretary to the king, "sweet Tomasillo," as he was called, was chosen as "the meetest messenger" to be sent to France with a love-letter and a jewel for the bride-elect, Henrietta Maria. Lord Holland reported to Prince Charles that his letter had been faithfully delivered by "sweet Tom Cary," and once again at least did this sweet gentleman cross the Channel with gifts from the prince to his princess. Charles I., on his accession, besides retaining Tom Carey as groom of his bed-chamber, heaped favours on him in the shape of grants of lands and money. Among these grants was that of the manor of Sunninghill, which was made in 1630. Thomas Carey was designated as ambassador in Venice in 1633, but he fell ill and died at Whitehall, April 9, 1634, and was buried in Westminster Abbey. He had married Margaret Smith, daughter and heiress of Sir Thomas Smith, Master of Requests, and by her he left three daughters, one of whom married Sir Thomas Draper, and brought him as her marriage-portion Sunninghill Park.

Thomas Carey, besides bearing a name vocally identical with that of Thomas Carew, and holding the post of groom of the bed-chamber, while the other was gentleman of the privy-chamber, contributed further to a possible confusion by being something of a poet. Henry Lawes set two of his compositions to music, as he did several by Thomas Carew, and he carefully distinguished in his published song-books between the son to the Earl of Monmouth, gentleman of the bed-chamber, and him of the privy-chamber. Mr. Hazlitt came to the conclusion that Lawes was mistaken in his attributions, principally on the ground that "in his translation of Puget La Serre's (*sic*) *Mirrour which flatters not* are some of Carey's metrical interpolations and additions which show him to have been utterly destitute of the poetical faculty." But the Carey who translated de la Serre's work was a third Thomas Carey, as is sufficiently shown by the title-page of his book: he was the son of Allen Carey, of Tower Hill, was admitted a student of Gray's Inn in 1627, and two years later was appointed gentleman-porter of the Tower.

Anthony à Wood says that Thomas Carey (son of the Earl of Monmouth) "proved afterwards a most ingenious poet and was author of several poems printed scatteredly in divers books." Unfortunately the only two poems certainly known to be of his authorship are the two mentioned which were set to music as his by Lawes, and were translated into Latin as his by Sir Richard Fanshawe,[1] and these are here reprinted (pp. 174—6). It would be rash to assert that any of the poems assigned to Thomas Carew was really the production of the other poet, but there was at any rate ample opportunity for error. But even if it be granted that the compositions of the two have always been kept distinct, as much cannot be said of their portraits. John Fry, the Bristol antiquarian, who published a selection of Carew's poems in 1816, promised a complete edition on which he had been at work more than four years, "to be illustrated with portraits of the authour and his wife from a rare medal by Warin." The book never appeared; but Varin's medallion portrait of Thomas Carey had already been engraved and issued to the world as the portrait of

[1] In *Il Pastor Fido: The Faithful Shepherd* with an addition of divers other poems. 1648.

Thomas Carew, albeit, the legend round the medal left no doubt as to the identity of the original, "Tho. Cary, R. Carol. Cubicular, aetatis suae 35, 1633." Thomas Carew was 38 years old in 1633 and was never *cubicularis*—of the bed-chamber. His portrait was painted by Vandyck, and hangs in Windsor Castle. Mr. Hazlitt used Varin's portrait of Carey for his edition of Carew, and took the liberty of altering the inscription.

The main story of Thomas Carey's life is thus fairly clear and well established, but although it proves that it was not Thomas Carew who owned Sunninghill Park and was dead in the spring of 1638, it naturally furnishes no additional evidence as to the exact time of the better-known poet's death. The tradition that it occurred in 1639, which is supported by the apparently posthumous publication of his poems in 1640, is contradicted in Clarendon's Life, where it is stated of Carew that "his glory was that after fifty years of life spent with less severity and exactness than it ought to have been, he died with the greatest remorse for that license and with the greatest manifestations of Christianity that his best friends could desire." If Carew had fifty years of life he must have lived till 1645, but there is, perhaps, no need to press the words closely, there being no reason for supposing that Clarendon kept accurate count of Carew's years. The story of his deathbed repentance seems to have been true, or is at any rate borne out by an anecdote, for which Isaak Walton made, or intended to make himself responsible, and which is found in his MS. collections for a life of Hales.[1] Thus it stands:

"Then was told this by Mr. Anthony Faringdon, and have heard it discussed by others, that Mr. Thomas Cary, a poet of note and a great libertine in his life and talk, and one that had in his youth been acquainted with Mr. Ha. sent for Mr. Hales to come to him in a dangerous fit of sickness and desired his advice and absolution, which Mr. Hales, upon a promise of amendment, gave him (this was I think in the country). But Mr. Cary came to London, fell to his own company and into a more visible scandalous life, and especially in his discourse, and he [being] taken very sick, that which proved his last, and being much troubled in mind, procured Mr. Ha. to come to him in this his sickness and agony of mind, desiring earnestly after a confession of many of his sins, to have his prayers and his absolution. Mr. Ha. told him he should have his prayers, but would by no means give him then either the sacrament or absolution."

Carew's illness in the country may have occurred at one of the houses he was in the habit of visiting, among which were Saxham; Wrest, the seat of the Grey family whence he wrote to his friend Gilbert N. (p. 120) apparently after some fighting expedition in the north; and West Horsley, the seat of Carew Raleigh, whither Suckling addressed a letter to the poet when ill. He would seem to have come to London to ask in vain for the ministrations of Hales and to die in fear, perhaps in King street, Westminster, where he lived or was staying (possibly at one

---

[1] The same story is told in Hunter's *Chorus Vatum* (Add. MS. 24,489) as having been related by Lady Salter "as a certain fact." Hales was tutor to Lady Salter's son.

of the inns for which the street was favourably known) when his friend and admirer, Davenant, addressed to him the verses to which allusion has been made. But no record has been found of the place of his death or of his burial.

Time has thus shrouded in a haze, which there is small hope of dispelling, the life and true character of Carew the man, and has left nothing but his poetical work and the Masque, produced by royal command for a Shrove Tuesday performance in 1634. The poems, notwithstanding the continually personal note which is struck throughout, are yet impersonal inasmuch as they reflect no particular type of mind, and might for anything that can be found in them to the contrary have been written by another man of equal ability, placed in totally different circumstances. Nothing else could be expected from verse which, far from being the spontaneous outburst of a distressed or joyous soul, was evidently for the most part well considered, carefully put together and highly polished. Suckling, whose verse has often every appearance of having been "knocked off," made pointed allusion to the contrary practice of his friend in the "Session of the Poets":

> Tom Carew came next but he had a fault
> That could not stand well with a laureate;
> His Muse was hide-bound and the issue of 's brain
> Was seldom brought forth but with trouble and pain.

Carew probably made no secret of the chronic constipation of his muse, and to judge from his lines to Ben Jonson (p. 90) seems to have regarded work smelling of the lamp as the best—

*c*

> Let them the dear expense of oil upbraid
> Suck'd by thy watchful lamp . . .
> Repine not at thy thrifty taper's waste
> That sleeks thy terser poems; nor is haste
> Praise but excuse . . .
>    \*     \*     \*     \*     \*
> Thy labour'd works shall live when Time devours
> The abortive offspring of their hasty hours.

Carew certainly "sleeked" his own lyric poems to their great advantage and with the happy result that the best of them are very perfect specimens of their kind. Many a courtly poet, addressing his mistress, was content, when he had lighted on what seemed a happy idea, to pad more or less apposite rhyme around it until a proper length was reached. Carew preferred to work out his idea and to turn out a poem every part of which seemed naturally joined to what went before or what followed, and so far he succeeded sometimes better than any earlier English poet had troubled to do. He worked in an appreciative age, and his verse acquired the popularity which some of it merited and has preserved. Perhaps no poems are to be found more often copied out in MS. commonplace books than those of Carew, and Davenant's jocular lines, anticipating the effect of his friend's death, bear witness to his place among the love-poets—

> "How glad and gaudy then will lovers be!
> For every lover that can verses read
> Hath been so injured by thy verse and thee
> Ten thousand-thousand times he wished thee dead."

And in these days when but few of us take the pains to transcribe what pleases the taste as we read, and anthologies have taken the place of the home-made commonplace books, there is no industrious

compiler of miscellaneous verse who can afford to
dispense with "Who that loves a rosy cheek," "Ask
me no more where Jove bestows," and "Give me
more love or more disdain." These favourites are
unimpeachable, but were it not for the demands on
the space of the anthologist and the necessity for a
display of the breadth of his reading, they need not
stand alone. "When thou poor excommunicate,"
"Now you have freely given me leave to love,"
"Kiss lovely Celia and be kind," "You that will a
wonder know," are all poems which in their kind are
not easily to be matched.

But Carew's standard was by no means uniformly
high. In view of his *Rapture* it can hardly be said
that he was incapable of a sustained effort, but in the
elegies, obsequies and other occasional pieces of verse,
written when something of the kind was expected of
him, or when he thought it was expected, he can
hardly be considered so successful as in his lyrics. He
was at all times a pupil in the school of Donne—as
who of his age was not?—but with a frequency
which he would scarcely have permitted himself after
the publication of Donne's poems he borrowed with
some freedom not merely the ideas of the master, but
his very words and manner of expression. When he
tried to follow Donne at a greater distance and to
invent something of his own on the same lines, he
became nearly ridiculous, not seeming to realize that
what was excusable, and sometimes admirable, in a
Donne was not permissible to a Carew. Such phrases
as "nest of spice" (= young woman), "clayey tene-

ment" (= human body), "mixed dew of briny sweet," "salt amorous rheum," "flood of pearly moisture" (all = tears), "stately pillars" (= Earl of Anglesey's legs), "brittle beauty," "repercussive sorceries" could only have been written down in the innocent belief that such modes of speech were praiseworthy and honourable to the begetter. But such blots are hardly so common as to be characteristic, and when all have been found there is still the indisputable fact that much which remains makes remarkably pretty reading.

## BIBLIOGRAPHICAL NOTE.

THE first published work of Carew (so far as is known) was this masque *Coelum Britanicum*, the title page of which runs thus: " *Coelum Brittanicum* / a / Masque at / Whitehall in / the Banquetting House / on Shrove Tuesday-night / the 18 of February / 1633 /. The Inventors / Tho: Carew. Inigo Jones / *Non habit ingenium; Cæsar sed jussit: habebo.*/ *Cur me posse negem posse quod ille putat.* / London / Printed for Thomas Walkley and are to be sold at his shop neare Whitehall / 1634."

The first printed edition of the Poems appeared in 1640 with the following title: POEMS / By / Thomas Carew / Esquire / One of the Gentlemen of the / Privie-Chamber and Sewer in / Ordinary to his Majesty /. London / Printed by I. D. for Thomas Walkley,/ and are to be sold at the signe of the / flying Horse, between Brittains / Burse, and York House / 1640 /. Appended is the masque, the pagination being continuous. The volume bears the *imprimatur* of Matthew Clay, April 29, 1640. Some copies of this edition were issued on larger paper than others.

In 1642 Walkley published a new edition with eight additional poems including one by Waller.

## xxxviii BIBLIOGRAPHICAL NOTE.

In 1651 a third edition was published for H.M., and tacked on after the masque were three additional poems.

A fourth edition "revised and enlarged" published in 1671 contains no more than is in that of 1651.

In the eighteenth century the Poems, etc., were reprinted once only, in 1772, with the addition of a more or less apocryphal life of the author and some notes which were mainly explanatory of classical allusions.

The present century has already seen four editions of Carew's works, besides a selection of his poems published in 1810 and edited by John Fry, of Bristol, who contemplated but did not bring out a complete edition.

The four complete editions are—

(*a*) A limited edition prepared by Thomas Maitland, a Lord of Session, and reprinted from the first edition with an appendix of poems added in 1642 and 1651.—1824.

(*b*) A paper-covered reprint issued with no editor's name by H. G. Clarke and Co.—1845.

(*c*) The Poems of Thomas Carew now first collected and edited with notes from the former editions and new notes and a memoir by W. Carew Hazlitt, the text formed from a collation of all the old printed copies and many early MSS.—1870.

(*d*) The Poems and Masque of Thomas Carew . . . with an introductory memoir, an Appendix of Unauthenticated Poems from MSS., Notes, and a Table of First Lines. Edited by Joseph Woodfall Ebsworth, M.A., F.S.A., etc.—1893.

All the editions enumerated above are naturally based on the original edition of 1640, the text of which has been carefully followed in the present edition. There are small variations in the succeeding early editions, but these have not been noted since they are manifestly due to careless printing and not to the corrections of a careful and sagacious editor. Mr. Hazlitt's edition (1870) gives an altered text occasionally, on the authority of some MS., but such authority is of small value when it cannot be proved that the MS. copy preceded the printed work. There are almost countless MS. copies of Carew's poems, but there is nothing to show that any of them was written before the publication of the poems in print, and when they present readings different from the printed text, the variation is generally obviously due to careless copying.

Both Mr. Hazlitt and Mr. Ebsworth included in their editions versions of some of the Psalms which are attributed to Carew in one of the Ashmole MSS., and also, it has been stated, in a MS. referred to by Mr. Hazlitt as the Wyburd MS. They are not here reprinted, as they possess no merit or interest, and it is always unsafe to trust the ascriptions of MSS.; there being, for instance, equal MS. authority for assigning the verses commencing "Drink to me only with thine eyes" to Thomas Carew as was relied upon by Mr. Hazlitt for crediting him with the Psalms. It seems safer to admit the evidence of Carew himself in his verses to Sandys,

> My unwash'd muse pollutes not things divine,
> Nor mingles her profaner notes with thine.

On the authority of the aforesaid Wyburd MS. Mr.

Hazlitt printed several copies of verses which it would be difficult to believe were written by Carew without much additional evidence. The authority for such poems (beyond those appearing in the editions of 1640, 1642 and 1651) as are reprinted in the present volume is stated in the notes.

\* \* \* \* \*

The poems in the original edition are preceded by the following

### ERRATES.

Page 5, line 4, *for* their *read* your ; p. 15, l. 3, *for* sent *r.* lent ; p. 43, l. 11, *for* it *r.* not ; p. 77, l. 3, *for* danke *r.* dampe ; p. 85, l. 7, *for* Souldiers *r.* Lovers ; p. 11, l. 15, *r.* I straight might feele ; p. 113, l. 17, *for* the *r.* that ; p. 122, l. 2, *for* where *r.* what ; p. 138, l. 3 *for* pastime *r.* passion ; p. 148, *for* circle *r.* sickle.

The pagination in this list is, of course, that of the original edition. The corrections have been incorporated in the present text.

# POEMS.

### THE SPRING.

Now that the winter's gone, the earth hath lost
Her snow-white robes; and now no more the frost
Candies the grass, or casts an icy cream
Upon the silver lake or crystal stream:
But the warm sun thaws the benumbed earth,     5
And makes it tender; gives a sacred birth
To the dead swallow; wakes in hollow tree
The drowsy cuckoo and the humble-bee.
Now do a choir of chirping minstrels bring,
In triumph to the world, the youthful spring:     10
The valleys, hills, and woods in rich array
Welcome the coming of the long'd-for May.
Now all things smile: only my love doth lower,
Nor hath the scalding noon-day sun the power
To melt that marble ice, which still doth hold     15
Her heart congeal'd, and makes her pity cold.
The ox, which lately did for shelter fly
Into the stall, doth now securely lie
In open fields; and love no more is made
By the fire-side, but in the cooler shade     20
Amyntas now doth with his Chloris sleep
Under a sycamore, and all things keep
  Time with the season: only she doth carry
  June in her eyes, in her heart January.

## TO A. L.

### PERSUASIONS TO LOVE.

Think not, 'cause men flattering say
You're fresh as April, sweet as May,
Bright as is the morning star,
That you are so; or, though you are,
Be not therefore proud, and deem      5
All men unworthy your esteem :
For, being so, you lose the pleasure
Of being fair, since that rich treasure
Of rare beauty and sweet feature
Was bestow'd on you by nature      10
To be enjoy'd; and 'twere a sin
There to be scarce, where she hath bin
So prodigal of her best graces.
Thus common beauties and mean faces
Shall have more pastime, and enjoy      15
The sport you lose by being coy.
Did the thing for which I sue
Only concern myself, not you;
Were men so framed as they alone
Reap'd all the pleasure, women none;      20
Then had you reason to be scant :
But 'twere a madness not to grant
That which affords (if you consent)

l. 2. *Fresh as Helen* in several MSS.

To you, the giver, more content
Than me, the beggar. Oh, then be  25
Kind to yourself, if not to me.
Starve not yourself, because you may
Thereby make me pine away;
Nor let brittle beauty make
You your wiser thoughts forsake;  30
For that lovely face will fail.
Beauty's sweet, but beauty's frail,
'Tis sooner past, 'tis sooner done,
Than summer's rain, or winter's sun;
Most fleeting, when it is most dear,  35
'Tis gone, while we but say 'tis here.
These curious locks, so aptly twined,
Whose every hair a soul doth bind,
Will change their auburn hue and grow
White and cold as winter's snow.  40
That eye, which now is Cupid's nest,
Will prove his grave, and all the rest
Will follow; in the cheek, chin, nose,
Nor lily shall be found, nor rose.
And what will then become of all  45
Those whom now you servants call?
Like swallows, when your summer's done,
They'll fly, and seek some warmer sun.
Then wisely choose one to your friend
Whose love may, when your beauties end,  50
Remain still firm: be provident,
And think, before the summer's spent,
Of following winter; like the ant,
In plenty hoard for time of scant.

Cull out, amongst the multitude 55
Of lovers, that seek to intrude
Into your favour, one that may
Love for an age, not for a day;
One that will quench your youthful fires,
And feed in age your hot desires. 60
For when the storms of time have moved
Waves on that cheek which was beloved,
When a fair lady's face is pined,
And yellow spread where red once shined;
When beauty, youth, and all sweets leave her, 65
Love may return, but lover never:
And old folks say there are no pains
Like itch of love in aged veins.
O love me, then, and now begin it,
Let us not lose this present minute; 70
For time and age will work that wrack
Which time or age shall ne'er call back.
The snake each year fresh skin resumes,
And eagles change their aged plumes;
The faded rose each spring receives 75
A fresh red tincture on her leaves:
But if your beauties once decay,
You never know a second May.
O then, be wise, and whilst your season
Affords you days for sport, do reason; 80
Spend not in vain your life's short hour,
But crop in time your beauty's flower,
Which will away, and doth together
Both bud and fade, both blow and wither.

### LIPS AND EYES.

In Celia's face a question did arise,
Which were more beautiful, her lips or eyes?
"We," said the eyes, "send forth those pointed darts
Which pierce the hardest adamantine hearts."
"From us," repli'd the lips, "proceed those blisses 5
Which lovers reap by kind words and sweet kisses."
Then wept the eyes, and from their springs did pour
Of liquid oriental pearl a shower;
Whereat the lips, moved with delight and pleasure,
Through a sweet smile unlock'd their pearly trea-
    sure 10
And bade Love judge, whether did add more grace
Weeping or smiling pearls to Celia's face.

## A DIVINE MISTRESS.

In Nature's pieces still I see
Some error that might mended be;
Something my wish could still remove,
Alter or add; but my fair love
Was framed by hands far more divine,　　5
For she hath every beauteous line.
Yet I had been far happier
Had Nature, that made me, made her.
Then likeness might (that love creates)
Have made her love what now she hates;　10
Yet, I confess, I cannot spare
From her just shape the smallest hair;
Nor need I beg from all the store
Of heaven for her one beauty more.
She hath too much divinity for me:　　15
You gods, teach her some more humanity.

### SONG.

#### A BEAUTIFUL MISTRESS.

If when the sun at noon displays
    His brighter rays,
    Thou but appear,
He then, all pale with shame and fear,
    Quencheth his light,   5
Hides his dark brow, flies from thy sight,
    And grows more dim,
Compared to thee, than stars to him.
If thou but show thy face again,
When darkness doth at midnight reign,   10
The darkness flies, and light is hurl'd
Round about the silent world:
So as alike thou driv'st away
Both light and darkness, night and day.

### A CRUEL MISTRESS.

WE read of kings and gods that kindly took
A pitcher fill'd with water from the brook ;
But I have daily tender'd without thanks
Rivers of tears that overflow their banks.
A slaughter'd bull will appease angry Jove,   5
A horse the sun, a lamb the god of love,
But she disdains the spotless sacrifice
Of a pure heart, that at her altar lies.
Vesta is not displeased, if her chaste urn
Do with repaired fuel ever burn ;   10
But my saint frowns, though to her honour'd name
I consecrate a never-dying flame.
Th' Assyrian king did none i' th' furnace throw
But those that to his image did not bow ;
With bended knees I daily worship her,   15
Yet she consumes her own idolater.
Of such a goddess no times leave record,
That burnt the temple where she was adored.

## SONG.

### MURDERING BEAUTY.

I'LL gaze no more on her bewitching face,
Since ruin harbours there in every place;
For my enchanted soul alike she drowns
With calms and tempests of her smiles and frowns.
I'll love no more those cruel eyes of hers,     5
Which, pleased or anger'd, still are murderers:
For if she dart, like lightning, through the air
Her beams of wrath, she kills me with despair:
If she behold me with a pleasing eye,
I surfeit with excess of joy, and die.     10

## MY MISTRESS COMMANDING ME TO RETURN HER LETTERS.

So grieves th' advent'rous merchant, when he throws
All the long toil'd-for treasure his ship stows
Into the angry main, to save from wrack
Himself and men, as I grieve to give back
These letters: yet so powerful is your sway     5
As if you bid me die, I must obey.
Go then, blest papers, you shall kiss those hands
That gave you freedom, but hold me in bands;
Which with a touch did give you life, but I,
Because I may not touch those hands, must die.   10
Methinks, as if they knew they should be sent
Home to their native soil from banishment;
I see them smile, like dying saints that know
They are to leave the earth and toward heaven go.
When you return, pray tell your sovereign     15
And mine, I gave you courteous entertain;
Each line received a tear, and then a kiss;
First bathed in that, it 'scaped unscorch'd from this:
I kiss'd it because your hand had been there;
But, 'cause it was not now, I shed a tear.     20
Tell her, no length of time, nor change of air,
No cruelty, disdain, absence, despair,
No, nor her steadfast constancy, can deter

l. 23. Add. MS. 10,309, *No, nor her constant scorn can once deter.*

My vassal heart from ever honouring her.
Though these be powerful arguments to prove        25
I love in vain, yet I must ever love.
Say, if she frown, when you that word rehearse,
Service in prose is oft called love in verse :
Then pray her, since I send back on my part
Her papers, she will send me back my heart.       30
If she refuse, warn her to come before
The god of love, whom thus I will implore :
" Trav'lling thy country's road, great god, I spied
By chance this lady, and walk'd by her side
From place to place, fearing no violence,         35
For I was well arm'd, and had made defence
In former fights 'gainst fiercer foes than she
Did at our first encounter seem to be.
But, going farther, every step reveal'd
Some hidden weapon till that time conceal'd ;     40
Seeing those outward arms, I did begin
To fear some greater strength was lodged within ;
Looking into her mind, I might survey
An host of beauties, that in ambush lay,
And won the day before they fought the field,     45
For I, unable to resist, did yield.
But the insulting tyrant so destroys
My conquer'd mind, my ease, my peace, my joys,
Breaks my sweet sleeps, invades my harmless rest,
Robs me of all the treasure of my breast,         50
Spares not my heart, nor yet a greater wrong,
For, having stol'n my heart, she binds my tongue.
But at the last her melting eyes unseal'd
My lips, enlarged my tongue : then I reveal'd

To her own ears the story of my harms, 55
Wrought by her virtues and her beauty's charms.
Now hear, just judge, an act of savageness;
When I complain, in hope to find redress,
She bends her angry brow, and from her eye
Shoots thousand darts; I then well hoped to die, 60
But in such sovereign balm Love dips his shot,
That, though they wound a heart, they kill it not.
She saw the blood gush forth from many a wound,
Yet fled, and left me bleeding on the ground,
Nor sought my cure, nor saw me since: 'tis true, 65
Absence and Time, two cunning leaches, drew
The flesh together, yet, sure, though the skin
Be closed without, the wound festers within.
Thus hath this cruel lady used a true
Servant and subject to herself and you; 70
Nor know I, great Love, if my life be lent
To show thy mercy or my punishment:
Since by the only magic of thy art
A lover still may live that wants his heart.
If this indictment fright her, so as she 75
Seem willing to return my heart to me,
But cannot find it (for perhaps it may,
'Mongst other trifling hearts, be out o' th' way);
If she repent and would make me amends,
Bid her but send me hers, and we are friends." 80

 l. 78. Add. MS. 10,309, '*Mongst other trifling things be thrown away.*

### SECRECY PROTESTED.

Fear not, dear love, that I'll reveal
Those hours of pleasure we two steal;
No eye shall see, nor yet the sun
Descry, what thou and I have done.
No ear shall hear our love, but we      5
Silent as the night will be;
The god of love himself (whose dart
Did first wound mine and then thy heart),
Shall never know that we can tell
What sweets in stol'n embraces dwell.   10
This only means may find it out:
If, when I die, physicians doubt
What caused my death, and there to view
Of all their judgments which was true,
Rip up my heart, oh! then, I fear,      15
The world will see thy picture there.

### A PRAYER TO THE WIND.

Go, thou gentle whispering wind,
Bear this sigh, and if thou find
Where my cruel fair doth rest
Cast it in her snowy breast,
So, inflamed by my desire,  5
It may set her heart afire.
Those sweet kisses thou shalt gain,
Will reward thee for thy pain;
Boldly light upon her lip,
There suck odours, and thence skip  10
To her bosom; lastly fall
Down, and wander over all.
Range about those ivory hills,
From whose every part distils
Amber dew; there spices grow,  15
There pure streams of nectar flow;
There perfume thyself, and bring
All those sweets upon thy wing.
As thou return'st, change by thy power
Every weed into a flower;  20
Turn each thistle to a vine,
Make the bramble eglantine;
For so rich a booty made,
Do but this, and I am paid.
Thou can'st with thy powerful blast  25
Heat apace, and cool as fast;

Thou can'st kindle hidden flame,
And again destroy the same:
Then, for pity, either stir
Up the fire of love in her, 30
That alike both flames may shine,
Or else quite extinguish mine.

## SONG.

### MEDIOCRITY IN LOVE REJECTED.

Give me more love or more disdain;
   The torrid or the frozen zone
Bring equal ease unto my pain,
   The temperate affords me none:
Either extreme of love or hate,        5
Is sweeter than a calm estate.

Give me a storm; if it be love,
   Like Danaë in that golden shower,
I swim in pleasure; if it prove
   Disdain, that torrent will devour     10
My vulture-hopes; and he's possess'd
Of heaven, that's but from hell released.
    Then crown my joys or cure my pain:
    Give me more love or more disdain.

## SONG.

### GOOD COUNSEL TO A YOUNG MAID.

Gaze not on thy beauty's pride,
Tender maid, in the false tide
That from lovers' eyes doth slide.

Let thy faithful crystal show
How thy colours come and go: 5
Beauty takes a foil from woe.

Love, that in those smooth streams lies
Under pity's fair disguise,
Will thy melting heart surprise.

Nets of passion's finest thread, 10
Snaring poems, will be spread,
All to catch thy maidenhead.

Then beware! for those that cure
Love's disease, themselves endure
For reward a calenture. 15

Rather let the lover pine,
Than his pale cheek should assign
A perpetual blush to thine.

## TO MY MISTRESS SITTING BY A RIVER'S SIDE.

### AN EDDY.

Mark, how yond eddy steals away
From the rude stream into the bay;
There, lock'd up safe, she doth divorce
Her waters from the channel's course,
And scorns the torrent that did bring 5
Her headlong from her native spring.
Now doth she with her new love play,
Whilst he runs murmuring away.
Mark how she courts the banks, whilst they
As amorously their arms display, 10
T' embrace, and clip her silver waves:
See how she strokes their sides, and craves
An entrance there, which they deny;
Whereat she frowns, threat'ning to fly
Home to her stream, and 'gins to swim 15
Backward, but from the channel's brim
Smiling returns into the creek,
With thousand dimples on her cheek.
  Be thou this eddy, and I'll make
My breast thy shore, where thou shalt take 20
Secure repose, and never dream
Of the quite forsaken stream;
Let him to the wide ocean haste,
There lose his colour, name, and taste:
Thou shalt save all, and, safe from him, 25
Within these arms for ever swim.

### SONG.

#### CONQUEST BY FLIGHT.

Ladies, fly from love's smooth tale,
Oaths steep'd in tears do oft prevail;
Grief is infectious, and the air
Inflame l with sighs will blast the fair.
Then stop your ears, when lovers cry,     5
Lest yourselves weep, when no soft eye
Shall with a sorrowing tear repay
That pity which you cast away.

Young men, fly, when beauty darts
Amorous glances at your hearts:     10
The fix'd mark gives the shooter aim,
And ladies' looks have power to maim;
Now 'twixt their lips, now in their eyes,
Wrapt in a smile or kiss, love lies:
Then fly betimes, for only they     15
Conquer love that run away.

l. 6. The original edition has *your selfe*.

### SONG.

#### TO MY INCONSTANT MISTRESS.

When thou, poor excommunicate
   From all the joys of love, shalt see
The full reward and glorious fate
   Which my strong faith shall purchase me,
   Then curse thine own inconstancy.     5

A fairer hand than thine shall cure
   That heart, which thy false oaths did wound;
And to my soul a soul more pure
   Than thine shall by Love's hand be bound,
   And both with equal glory crown'd.     10

Then shalt thou weep, entreat, complain
   To Love, as I did once to thee;
When all thy tears shall be as vain
   As mine were then, for thou shalt be
   Damn'd for thy false apostacy.     15

## SONG.

### PERSUASIONS TO ENJOY.

If the quick spirits in your eye
    Now languish and anon must die;
If every sweet and every grace
Must fly from that forsaken face;
    Then, Celia, let us reap our joys     5
    Ere time such goodly fruit destroys.

Or, if that golden fleece must grow
For ever free from aged snow;
If those bright suns must know no shade,
Nor your fresh beauties ever fade;     10
Then fear not, Celia, to bestow
What, still being gather'd, still must grow.
    Thus, either Time his sickle brings
    In vain, or else in vain his wings.

## A DEPOSITION FROM LOVE.

I was foretold your rebel sex
    Nor love nor pity knew;
And with what scorn you use to vex
    Poor hearts that humbly sue.
Yet I believed, to crown our pain,
    Could we the fortress win,
The happy lover sure should gain
    A paradise within:
I thought Love's plagues, like dragons, sat
Only to fright us at the gate.

But I did enter, and enjoy
    What happy lovers prove;
For I could kiss, and sport, and toy,
    And taste those sweets of love,
Which, had they but a lasting state,
    Or if in Celia's breast
The force of love might not abate,
    Jove were too mean a guest:
But now her breach of faith far more
Afflicts, than did her scorn before.

Hard fate! to have been once possess'd
    As victor of a heart,
Achieved with labour and unrest,
    And then forced to depart.
If the stout foe will not resign,
    When I besiege a town,
I lose but what was never mine;
    But he that is cast down
From enjoy'd beauty, feels a woe
Only deposed kings can know.

## INGRATEFUL BEAUTY THREATENED.

KNOW, Celia, since thou art so proud,
  'Twas I that gave thee thy renown;
Thou had'st in the forgotten crowd
  Of common beauties lived unknown,
Had not my verse exhaled thy name,      5
And with it imp'd the wings of Fame.

That killing power is none of thine:
  I gave it to thy voice and eyes;
Thy sweets, thy graces, all are mine;
  Thou art my star, shin'st in my skies:   10
Then dart not from thy borrow'd sphere
Lightning on him that fix'd thee there.

Tempt me with such affrights no more,
  Lest what I made I uncreate;
Let fools thy mystic forms adore,      15
  I'll know thee in thy mortal state:
Wise poets that wrapp'd Truth in tales,
Knew her themselves through all her veils.

### DISDAIN RETURNED.

He that loves a rosy cheek,
   Or a coral lip admires,
Or from star-like eyes doth seek
   Fuel to maintain his fires;
As old Time makes these decay,     5
So his flames must waste away.

But a smooth and steadfast mind,
   Gentle thoughts and calm desires,
Hearts with equal love combined,
   Kindle never-dying fires.     10
Where these are not, I despise
Lovely cheeks, or lips, or eyes.

No tears, Celia, now shall win
   My resolved heart to return;
I have search'd thy soul within,     15
   And find nought but pride and scorn:
I have learn'd thy arts, and now
Can disdain as much as thou.
   Some power in my revenge convey
   That love to her I cast away.     20

## A LOOKING-GLASS.

THAT flatt'ring glass, whose smooth face wears
Your shadow, which a sun appears,
Was once a river of my tears.

About your cold heart they did make
A circle, where the briny lake 5
Congeal'd into a crystal cake.

Gaze no more on that killing eye,
For fear the native cruelty
Doom you, as it doth all, to die:

For fear lest the fair object move 10
Your froward heart to fall in love:
Then you yourself my rival prove.

Look rather on my pale cheeks pined,
There view your beauties, there you'll find
A fair face, but a cruel mind. 15

Be not for ever frozen, coy!
One beam of love will soon destroy
And melt that ice to floods of joy.

### AN ELEGY ON THE LA: PEN:
### SENT TO MY MISTRESS OUT OF FRANCE.

LET him, who from his tyrant mistress did
This day receive his cruel doom, forbid
His eyes to weep that loss, and let him here
Open those flood-gates to bedew this bier;
So shall those drops, which else would be but brine,  5
Be turn'd to manna, falling on her shrine.
Let him who, banish'd far from her dear sight,
Whom his soul loves, doth in that absence write
Or lines of passion or some powerful charms,
To vent his own grief or unlock her arms,  10
Take off his pen, and in sad verse bemoan
This general sorrow, and forget his own.
So may those verses live, which else must die;
For though the Muses give eternity
When they embalm with verse, yet she could give  15
Life unto that Muse by which others live.
Oh, pardon me, fair soul, that boldly have
Dropp'd though but one tear on thy silent grave,
And writ on that earth, which such honour had,
To clothe that flesh wherein thyself was clad.  20

And pardon me, sweet saint, whom I adore,
That I this tribute pay out of the store
Of lines and tears that's only due to thee.
Oh, do not think it new idolatry;
Though you are only sovereign of this land, 25
Yet universal losses may command
A subsidy from every private eye,
And press each pen to write; so to supply
And feed the common grief.  If this excuse
Prevail not, take these tears to your own use, 30
As shed for you: for when I saw her die,
I then did think on your mortality.
For since nor virtue, will, nor beauty, could
Preserve from Death's hand this their heavenly mould,
Where they were framed all, and where they dwelt, 35
I then knew you must die too, and did melt
Into these tears; but, thinking on that day,
And when the gods resolved to take away
A saint from us, I that did know what dearth
There was of such good souls upon the earth, 40
Began to fear lest Death, their officer,
Might have mistook and taken thee for her:
So had'st thou robb'd us of that happiness
Which she in heaven and I in thee possess.
But what can heaven to her glory add? 45
The praises she hath dead, living she had;
To say she's now an angel is no more
Praise than she had, for she was one before.
Which of the saints can show more votaries
Than she had here?  Even those that did despise 50
The angels, and may her, now she is one,

Did, whilst she lived, with pure devotion
Adore and worship her: her virtues had
All honour here, for this world was too bad
To hate or envy her; these cannot rise 55
So high as to repine at deities:
But now she's 'mongst her fellow-saints, they may
Be good enough to envy her: this way
There's loss i' th' change 'twixt heaven and earth, if she
Should leave her servants here below to be 60
Hated of her competitors above.
But sure her matchless goodness needs must move
Those blest souls to admire her excellence;
By this means only can her journey hence
To heaven prove gain, if, as she was but here 65
Worshipp'd by men, she be by angels there.
But I must weep no more over this urn,
My tears to their own channel must return;
And having ended these sad obsequies,
My Muse must back to her old exercise, 70
To tell the story of my martyrdom.
But oh, thou idol of my soul, become
Once pitiful, that she may change her style,
Dry up her blubber'd eyes, and learn to smile.
Rest then, blest soul! for, as ghosts fly away 75
When the shrill cock proclaims the infant day,
So must I hence, for lo! I see from far
The minions of the Muses coming are,
Each of them bringing to thy sacred hearse
In either eye a tear, each hand a verse. 80

## TO MY MISTRESS IN ABSENCE.

Though I must live here, and by force
Of your command suffer divorce;
Though I am parted, yet my mind,
That's more myself, still stays behind.
I breathe in you, you keep my heart,        5
'Twas but a carcase that did part.
Then though our bodies are disjoin'd,
As things that are to place confined,
Yet let our boundless spirits meet,
And in love's sphere each other greet;      10
There let us work a mystic wreath,
Unknown unto the world beneath:
There let our clasp'd loves sweetly twin,
There let our secret thoughts unseen
Like nets be weaved and inter-twined,       15
Wherewith we'll catch each other's mind.
There, whilst our souls do sit and kiss,
Tasting a sweet and subtle bliss
(Such as gross lovers cannot know
Whose hands and lips meet here below),      20
Let us look down, and mark what pain
Our absent bodies here sustain,
And smile to see how far away
The one doth from the other stray;
Yet burn and languish with desire           25
To join and quench their mutual fire;

There let us joy to see from far
Our emulous flames at loving war,
Whilst both with equal lustre shine,
Mine bright as yours, yours bright as mine. 30
There, seated in those heavenly bowers,
We'll cheat the lag and ling'ring hours,
Making our bitter absence sweet,
Till souls and bodies both may meet.


### TO HER IN ABSENCE.

#### A SHIP.

Toss'd in a troubled sea of griefs, I float
Far from the shore, in a storm-beaten boat;
Where my sad thoughts do, like the compass, show
The several points from which cross-winds do blow.
My heart doth, like the needle, touch'd with love, 5
Still fix'd on you, point which way I would move;
You are the bright pole-star, which, in the dark
Of this long absence, guides my wand'ring bark;
Love is the pilot, but, o'er-come with fear
Of your displeasure, dares not homewards steer. 10
My fearful hope hangs on my trembling sail,
Nothing is wanting but a gentle gale,
Which pleasant breath must blow from your sweet lip:
Bid it but move, and quick as thought this ship
Into your arms, which are my port, will fly, 15
Where it for ever shall at anchor lie.

## SONG.

### ETERNITY OF LOVE PROTESTED.

How ill doth he deserve a lover's name
    Whose pale weak flame
    Cannot retain
His heat, in spite of absence or disdain;
But doth at once, like paper set on fire    5
    Burn and expire!
True love can never change his seat,
Nor did he ever love that could retreat.

That noble flame, which my breast keeps alive,
    Shall still survive    10
    When my soul's fled;
Nor shall my love die, when my body's dead;
That shall wait on me to the lower shade,
    And never fade:
My very ashes in their urn    15
Shall, like a hallow'd lamp, for ever burn.

## UPON SOME ALTERATIONS IN MY MISTRESS, AFTER MY DEPARTURE INTO FRANCE.

Oh, gentle love, do not forsake the guide
Of my frail bark, on which the swelling tide
      Of ruthless pride
Doth beat and threaten wrack from every side.
Gulfs of disdain do gape to overwhelm
This boat, nigh sunk with grief, whilst at the helm
      Despair commands;
And, round about, the shifting sands
Of faithless love and false inconstancy,
      With rocks of cruelty,
Stop up my passage to the neighbour lands.

My sighs have raised those winds, whose fury bears
My sails o'erboard, and in their place spreads tears;
      And from my tears
This sea is sprung, where nought but death appears.
A misty cloud of anger hides the light
Of my fair star; and everywhere black night
      Usurps the place
Of those bright rays, which once did grace
My forth-bound ship: but when it could no more
      Behold the vanish'd shore,
In the deep flood she drown'd her beamy face.

## GOOD COUNSEL TO A YOUNG MAID.

When you the sun-burnt pilgrim see
   Fainting with thirst, haste to the springs;
Mark how at first with bended knee
   He courts the crystal nymphs, and flings
His body to the earth, where he       5
Prostrate adores the flowing deity.

But when his sweaty face is drench'd
   In her cool waves, when from her sweet
Bosom his burning thirst is quench'd,
   Then mark how with disdainful feet    10
He kicks her banks, and from the place
That thus refresh'd him, moves with sullen pace.

So shalt thou be despised, fair maid,
   When, by the sated lover tasted,
What first he did with tears invade    15
   Shall afterwards with scorn be wasted:
When all thy virgin-springs grow dry,
When no streams shall be left but in thine eye.

### CELIA BLEEDING.

#### TO THE SURGEON.

FOND man, that canst believe her blood
   Will from those purple channels flow;
Or that the pure untainted flood
   Can any foul distemper know;
Or that thy weak steel can incise         5
The crystal case wherein it lies:

Know, her quick blood, proud of his seat,
   Runs dancing through her azure veins;
Whose harmony no cold nor heat
   Disturbs, whose hue no tincture stains:   10
And the hard rock, wherein it dwells,
The keenest darts of love repels.

But thou repli'st "Behold, she bleeds!"
   Fool! thou'rt deceived, and dost not know
The mystic knot whence this proceeds,     15
   How lovers in each other grow:
Thou struck'st her arm, but 'twas my heart
Shed all the blood, felt all the smart.

## TO T. H., A LADY RESEMBLING MY MISTRESS.

Fair copy of my Celia's face,
Twin of my soul, thy perfect grace
Claims in my love an equal place.

Disdain not a divided heart,
Though all be hers, you shall have part:   5
Love is not tied to rules of art.

For as my soul first to her flew,
Yet stay'd with me, so now 'tis true
It dwells with her, though fled to you.

Then entertain this wand'ring guest,   10
And if not love, allow it rest:
It left not, but mistook, the nest.

Nor think my love, or your fair eyes,
Cheaper, 'cause from the sympathies
You hold with her these flames arise.   15

To lead or brass, or some such bad
Metal, a prince's stamp may add
That value which it never had;

But to the pure refined ore
The stamp of kings imparts no more   20
Worth than the metal held before.

Only the image gives the rate
To subjects ; in a foreign state
'Tis prized as much for its own weight.

So though all other hearts resign 25
To your pure worth, yet you have mine
Only because you are her coin.

## TO SAXHAM.

Though frost and snow lock'd from mine eyes
That beauty which without door lies,
Thy gardens, orchards, walks, that so
I might not all thy pleasures know ;
Yet, Saxham, thou within thy gate 5
Art of thyself so delicate,
So full of native sweets, that bless
Thy roof with inward happiness,
As neither from, nor to thy store
Winter takes aught, or spring adds more. 10
The cold and frozen air had sterved
Much poor, if not by thee preserved,
Whose prayers have made thy table blest
With plenty, far above the rest.

The season hardly did afford 15
Coarse cates unto thy neighbours' board,
Yet thou hadst dainties, as the sky
Had only been thy volary;
Or else the birds, fearing the snow
Might to another deluge grow, 20
The pheasant, partridge, and the lark
Flew to thy house, as to the Ark.
The willing ox of himself came
Home to the slaughter with the lamb,
And every beast did thither bring 25
Himself, to be an offering.
The scaly herd more pleasure took,
Bathed in thy dish than in the brook;
Water, earth, air, did all conspire
To pay their tributes to thy fire, 30
Whose cherishing flames themselves divide
Through every room, where they deride
The night and cold abroad; whilst they,
Like suns within, keep endless day.
Those cheerful beams send forth their light 35
To all that wander in the night,
And seem to beckon from aloof
The weary pilgrim to thy roof,
Where if, refresh'd, he will away,
He's fairly welcome; or, if stay, 40
Far more; which he shall hearty find
Both from the master and the hind:
The stranger's welcome each man there
Stamp'd on his cheerful brow doth wear.

Nor doth this welcome or his cheer 45
Grow less, 'cause he stays longer here:
There's none observes, much less repines,
How often this man sups or dines.
Thou hast no porter at thy door
T' examine or keep back the poor; 50
Nor locks nor bolts: thy gates have bin
Made only to let strangers in;
Untaught to shut, they do not fear
To stand wide open all the year,
Careless who enters, for they know 55
Thou never didst deserve a foe:
And as for thieves, thy bounty's such,
They cannot steal, thou giv'st so much.

## UPON A RIBBON.

This silken wreath, which circles in mine arm,
Is but an emblem of that mystic charm
Wherewith the magic of your beauties binds
My captive soul, and round about it winds
Fetters of lasting love. This hath entwined          5
My flesh alone; that hath empaled my mind.
Time may wear out these soft weak bands, but those
Strong chains of brass Fate shall not discompose.
This holy relic may preserve my wrist,
But my whole frame doth by that power subsist :     10
To that my prayers and sacrifice, to this
I only pay a superstitious kiss.
This but the idol, that's the deity;
Religion there is due; here, ceremony;
That I receive by faith, this but in trust;         15
Here I may tender duty: there, I must;
This order as a layman I may bear,
But I become Love's priest when that I wear;
This moves like air; that as the centre stands;
That knot your virtue tied; this but your hands;    20
That, Nature framed; but this was made by art;
This makes my arm your prisoner; that, my heart.

## TO THE KING, AT HIS ENTRANCE INTO SAXHAM, BY MASTER JOHN CROFTS.

SIR,
  Ere you pass this threshold, stay,
And give your creature leave to pay
Those pious rites, which unto you,
As to our household gods, are due.
Instead of sacrifice, each breast          5
Is like a flaming altar drest
With zealous fires, which from pure hearts
Love mix'd with loyalty imparts.
Incense nor gold have we, yet bring
As rich and sweet an offering;             10
And such as doth both these express,
Which is our humble thankfulness;
By which is paid the all we owe
To gods above, or men below.
The slaughter'd beast, whose flesh should feed 15
The hungry flames, we for pure need
Dress for your supper; and the gore
Which should be dash'd on every door,
We change into the lusty blood
Of youthful vines, of which a flood        20
Shall sprightly run through all your veins,
First to your health, then your fair train's.

We shall want nothing but good fare,
To show your welcome and our care;
Such rarities, that come from far, 25
From poor men's houses banish'd are:
Yet we'll express in homely cheer
How glad we are to see you here.
We'll have whate'er the season yields
Out of the neighbouring woods and fields; 30
For all the dainties of your board
Will only be what those afford;
And, having supp'd, we may perchance
Present you with a country dance.

  Thus much your servants, that bear sway 35
Here in your absence, bade me say,
And beg, besides, you'ld hither bring
Only the mercy of a king,
And not the greatness: since they have
A thousand faults must pardon crave, 40
But nothing that is fit to wait
Upon the glory of your state.
Yet your gracious favour will,
They hope, as heretofore, shine still
On their endeavours, for they swore 45
Should Jove descend, they could no more.

## UPON THE SICKNESS OF E. S.

Must she then languish, and we sorrow thus,
And no kind god help her, nor pity us?
Is justice fled from heaven?  Can that permit
A foul deformed ravisher to sit
Upon her virgin cheek, and pull from thence         5
The rose-buds in their maiden excellence?
To spread cold paleness on her lips, and chase
The frighted rubies from their native place?
To lick up with his searching flames a flood
Of dissolved coral, flowing in her blood;            10
And with the damps of his infectious breath
Print on her brow moist characters of death?
Must the clear light, 'gainst course of nature, cease
In her fair eyes, and yet the flames increase?
Must fevers shake this goodly tree, and all          15
That ripen'd fruit from the fair branches fall,
Which princes have desired to taste?  Must she,
Who hath preserved her spotless chastity
From all solicitation, now at last
By agues and diseases be embraced?                   20
Forbit it, holy Dian! else who shall
Pay vows, or let one grain of incense fall
On thy neglected altars, if thou bless
No better this thy zealous votaress?

Haste then, O maiden goddess, to her aid;  25
Let on thy quiver her pale cheek be laid,
And rock her fainting body in thine arms;
Then let the god of music with still charms
Her restless eyes in peaceful slumbers close,
And with soft strains sweeten her calm repose.  30
Cupid, descend! and whilst Apollo sings,
Fanning the cool air with thy panting wings
Ever supply her with refreshing wind;
Let thy fair mother with her tresses bind
Her labouring temples, with whose balmy sweat  35
She shall perfume her hairy coronet,
Whose precious drops shall upon every fold
Hang like rich pearls about a wreath of gold;
Her looser locks, as they unbraided lie,
Shall spread themselves into a canopy,  40
Under whose shadow let her rest secure
From chilling cold or burning calenture:
Unless she freeze with ice of chaste desires,
Or holy Hymen kindle nuptial fires:
And when at last Death comes to pierce her heart,  45
Convey into his hand thy golden dart.

## A NEW-YEAR'S SACRIFICE.

### TO LUCINDA.

Those that can give, open their hands this day;
Those that cannot, yet hold them up to pray,
That health may crown the seasons of this year,
And mirth dance round the circle; that no tear,
Unless of joy, may with its briny dew       5
Discolour on your cheek the rosy hue;
That no access of years presume to abate
Your beauties' ever-flourishing estate.
Such cheap and vulgar wishes I could lay
As trivial off'rings at your feet this day,       10
But that it were apostacy in me
To send a prayer to any deity
But your divine self, who have power to give
Those blessings unto others, such as live
Like me, by the sole influence of your eyes,       15
Whose fair aspects govern our destinies.
   Such incense, vows, and holy rites as were
To the involved serpent of the year
Paid by Egyptian priests, lay I before
Lucinda's sacred shrine, whilst I adore       20
Her beauteous eyes, and her pure altars dress
With gums and spice of humble thankfulness.
   So may my goddess from her heaven inspire
My frozen bosom with a Delphic fire;
And then the world shall, by that glorious flame, 25
Behold the blaze of thy immortal name.

### SONG.

#### TO ONE WHO, WHEN I PRAISED MY MISTRESS' BEAUTY, SAID I WAS BLIND.

WONDER not, though I am blind,
  For you must be
Dark in your eyes or in your mind,
  If, when you see
Her face, you prove not blind like me.  5
If the powerful beams that fly
  From her eye,
And those amorous sweets that lie
Scatter'd in each neighbouring part,
Find a passage to your heart;  10
Then you'll confess your mortal sight
Too weak for such a glorious light:
For if her graces you discover,
You grow, like me, a dazzled lover:
But if those beauties you not spy,  15
Then are you blinder far than I.

## SONG.

### TO MY MISTRESS, I BURNING IN LOVE.

I BURN; and cruel you, in vain
Hope to quench me with disdain;
If from your eyes those sparkles came
That have kindled all this flame,
What boots it me, though now you shroud   5
Those fierce comets in a cloud?
Since all the flames that I have felt
Could your snow yet never melt:
Nor can your snow, though you should take
Alps into your bosom, slake   10
The heat of my enamour'd heart.
But, with wonder, learn Love's art:
No seas of ice can cool desire,
Equal flames must quench Love's fire.
Then, think not that my heat can die,   15
Till you burn as well as I.

## SONG.

### TO HER AGAIN, SHE BURNING IN A FEVER.

Now she burns as well as I,
Yet my heat can never die;
She burns that never knew desire,
She that was ice, she that was fire,
She, whose cold heart chaste thoughts did arm 5
So as Love's flames could never warm
The frozen bosom where it dwelt,
She burns, and all her beauties melt.
She burns, and cries, "Love's fires are mild;
Fevers are God's; he's a child." 10
Love! let her know the difference
'Twixt the heat of soul and sense:
Touch her with thy flames divine,
So shalt thou quench her fire, and mine.

l. 4. *that was fire.* So the editions: the sense seems to require Hazlitt's emendation 'now is.'

### UPON THE KING'S SICKNESS.

SICKNESS, the minister of Death, doth lay
So strong a siege against our brittle clay,
As, whilst it doth our weak forts singly win,
It hopes at length to take all mankind in.
First it begins upon the womb to wait, 5
And doth the unborn child there uncreate;
Then rocks the cradle where the infant lies,
Where, ere it fully be alive, it dies;
It never leaves fond youth, until it have
Found or an early or a later grave; 10
By thousand subtle sleights from heedless man
It cuts the short allowance of a span;
And where both sober life and art combine
To keep it out, age makes them both resign.
Thus, by degrees, it only gain'd of late 15
The weak, the aged, or intemperate.
But now the tyrant hath found out a way
By which the sober, strong, and young decay;
Ent'ring his royal limbs that is our head,
Through us, his mystic limbs, the pain is spread; 20
That man that doth not feel his part hath none
In any part of his dominion;
If he hold land, that earth is forfeited,
And he unfit on any ground to tread.

This grief is felt at Court, where it doth move   25
Through every joint, like the true soul of love.
All those fair stars, that do attend on him,
Whence they derived their light, wax pale and dim;
That ruddy morning beam of Majesty,
Which should the sun's eclipsed light supply,   30
Is overcast with mists, and in the lieu
Of cheerful rays sends us down drops of dew.
That curious form, made of an earth refined,
At whose blest birth the gentle planets shined
With fair aspects, and sent a glorious flame   35
To animate so beautiful a frame,
That darling of the gods and men doth wear
A cloud on 's brow, and in his eye a tear.
And all the rest, save when his dread command
Doth bid them move, like lifeless statues stand.   40
So full a grief, so generally worn,
Shows a good king is sick, and good men mourn.

## SONG.

### TO A LADY, NOT YET ENJOYED BY HER HUSBAND.

Come, Celia, fix thine eyes on mine,
   And through those crystals our souls flitting
Shall a pure wreath of eye-beams twine,
   Our loving hearts together knitting.
Let eaglets the bright sun survey,      5
Though the blind mole discern not day.

When clear Aurora leaves her mate,
   The light of her grey eyes despising,
Yet all the world doth celebrate
   With sacrifice her fair up-rising.      10
Let eaglets the bright sun survey,
Though the blind mole discern not day.

A dragon kept the golden fruit,
   Yet he those dainties never tasted;
As others pined in the pursuit,      15
   So he himself with plenty wasted.
Let eaglets the bright sun survey,
Though the blind mole discern not day.

### SONG.

#### THE WILLING PRISONER TO HIS MISTRESS.

LET fools great Cupid's yoke disdain,
   Loving their own wild freedom better;
Whilst, proud of my triumphant chain,
   I sit, and court my beauteous fetter.

Her murd'ring glances, snaring hairs,      5
   And her bewitching smiles so please me,
As he brings ruin, that repairs
   The sweet afflictions that disease me.

Hide not those panting balls of snow
   With envious veils from my beholding;   10
Unlock those lips their pearly row
   In a sweet smile of love unfolding.

And let those eyes, whose motion wheels
   The restless fate of every lover,
Survey the pains my sick heart feels,     15
   And wounds themselves have made discover.

## A FLY THAT FLEW INTO MY MISTRESS' EYE.

WHEN this fly lived, she used to play
In the sunshine all the day;
Till, coming near my Celia's sight,
She found a new and unknown light,
So full of glory as it made 5
The noon-day sun a gloomy shade.
Then this amorous fly became
My rival and did court my flame;
She did from hand to bosom skip,
And from her breath, her cheek, and lip, 10
Suck'd all the incense and the spice,
And grew a bird of paradise.
At last into her eye she flew,
There, scorch'd in flames and drown'd in dew,
Like Phaethon from the sun's sphere, 15
She fell, and with her dropp'd a tear,
Of which a pearl was straight composed,
Wherein her ashes lie enclosed.
Thus she received from Celia's eye
Funeral flame, tomb, obsequy. 20

### SONG.

#### CELIA SINGING.

HARK, how my Celia with the choice
Music of her hand and voice
Stills the loud wind, and makes the wild
Incensed boar and panther mild.
Mark how those statues like men move,   5
Whilst men with wonder statues prove.
This stiff rock bends to worship her;
That idol turns idolater.

Now, see how all the new-inspired
Images with love are fired;   10
Hark how the tender marble groans,
And all the late transformed stones
Court the fair nymph, with many a tear,
Which she, more stony than they were,
Beholds with unrelenting mind;   15
Whilst they, amazed to see combined
Such matchless beauty with disdain,
Are all turn'd into stones again.

## SONG.

### CELIA SINGING.

You that think Love can convey
    No other way
But through the eyes into the heart
    His fatal dart,
Close up those casements, and but hear    5
    This Siren sing;
    And on the wing
Of her sweet voice it shall appear
That Love can enter at the ear.

Then unveil your eyes : behold     10
    The curious mould
Where that voice dwells ; and, as we know
    When the cocks crow,
    We freely may
    Gaze on the day,     15
So may you, when the music's done,
Awake and see the rising sun.

## SONG.

### TO ONE THAT DESIRED TO KNOW MY MISTRESS.

    Seek not to know my love, for she
    Hath vow'd her constant faith to me;
    Her mild aspects are mine, and thou
    Shalt only find a stormy brow:
    For if her beauty stir desire           5
    In me, her kisses quench the fire.
    Or I can to love's fountain go,
    Or dwell upon her hills of snow;
    But when thou burn'st, she shall not spare
    One gentle breath to cool the air;      10
    Thou shalt not climb those Alps, nor spy
    Where the sweet springs of Venus lie.
    Search hidden Nature and there find
    A treasure to enrich thy mind;
    Discover arts not yet reveal'd,        15
    But let my mistress live conceal'd:
    Though men by knowledge wiser grow,
    Yet here 'tis wisdom not to know.

## IN THE PERSON OF A LADY TO HER INCONSTANT SERVANT.

WHEN on the altar of my hand,
   Bedew'd with many a kiss and tear,
Thy now revolted heart did stand
   An humble martyr, thou didst swear
     Thus (and the god of love did hear): 5
" By those bright glances of thine eye,
Unless thou pity me, I die."

When first those perjured lips of thine,
   Be-paled with blasting sighs, did seal
Their violated faith on mine, 10
   From the soft bosom that did heal
     Thee, thou my melting heart didst steal:
My soul, inflamed with thy false breath,
Poison'd with kisses, suck'd in death.

Yet I nor hand nor lip will move, 15
   Revenge or mercy to procure
From the offended god of love:
   My curse is fatal, and my pure
     Love shall beyond thy scorn endure:
If I implore the gods, they'll find 20
Thee too ingrateful, me too kind.

## TRUCE IN LOVE INTREATED.

No more, blind god ! for see, my heart
Is made thy quiver, where remains
No void place for another dart ;
And, alas ! that conquest gains
Small praise, that only brings away     5
A tame and unresisting prey.

Behold a nobler foe, all arm'd,
Defies thy weak artillery,
That hath thy bow and quiver charm'd,
A rebel beauty, conquering thee :     10
If thou dar'st equal combat try,
Wound her, for 'tis for her I die.

## TO MY RIVAL.

HENCE, vain intruder, haste away!
Wash not with thy unhallow'd brine
The footsteps of my Celia's shrine;
Nor on her purer altars lay
Thy empty words, accents that may          5
   Some looser dame to love incline:
   She must have offerings more divine;
Such pearly drops, as youthful May
Scatters before the rising day;
   Such smooth soft language, as each line  10
Might stroke an angry god, or stay
   Jove's thunder, make the hearers pine
With envy: do this, thou shalt be
Servant to her, rival to me.

## BOLDNESS IN LOVE.

MARK how the bashful morn in vain
Courts the amorous marigold,
With sighing blasts and weeping rain,
Yet she refuses to unfold.
But when the planet of the day　　　　5
Approacheth with his powerful ray,
Then she spreads, then she receives
His warmer beams into her virgin leaves.
So shalt thou thrive in love, fond boy;
If thy tears and sighs discover　　　　10
Thy grief, thou never shalt enjoy
The just reward of a bold lover.
But when with moving accents thou
Shalt constant faith and service vow,
Thy Celia shall receive those charms　　　　15
With open ears, and with unfolded arms.

## A PASTORAL DIALOGUE.

### CELIA : CLEON.

    As Celia rested in the shade
        With Cleon by her side,
    The swain thus courted the young maid,
        And thus the nymph replied.

*Cleon.* Sweet ! let thy captive fetters wear     5
        Made of thine arms and hands ;
    Till such as thraldom scorn, or fear,
        Envy those happy bands.

*Celia.* Then thus my willing arms I wind
        About thee, and am so     10
    Thy pris'ner, for myself I bind,
        Until I let thee go.

*Cleon.* Happy that slave whom the fair foe
        Ties in so soft a chain.
*Celia.* Far happier I, but that I know     15
        Thou wilt break loose again.

*Cleon.* By thy immortal beauties, never !
   *Celia.* Frail as thy love 's thine oath.
*Cleon.* Though beauty fade, my faith lasts ever.
   *Celia.* Time will destroy them both.     20

*Cleon.* I dote not on thy snow-white skin.
   *Celia.* What then? *Cl.* Thy purer mind.
*Celia.* It loved too soon. *Cl.* Thou had'st not bin
     So fair, if not so kind.

*Celia.* Oh strange vain fancy! *Cl.* But yet true.  25
   *Celia.* Prove it! *Cleon.* Then make a braid
     Of those loose flames that circle you,
     My suns, and yet your shade.

*Celia.* 'Tis done. *Cl.* Now give it me. *Cel.* Thus thou
     Shalt thine own error find ;     30
   If these were beauties, I am now
     Less fair, because more kind.

*Cleon.* You shall confess you err : that hair,
     Shall it not change the hue,
   Or leave the golden mountain bare?     35
*Celia.* Ay me! it is too true.

*Cleon.* But this small wreath shall ever stay
     In its first native prime ;
   And smiling when the rest decay,
     The triumphs sing of time.     40

*Celia.* Then let me cut from thy fair grove
    One branch, and let that be
An emblem of eternal love,
    For such is mine to thee.

*Cleon.* Thus are we both redeem'd from time      45
    I by thy grace. *Celia.* And I
Shall live in thy immortal rhyme,
    Until the Muses die.

*Cleon.* By heaven! *Celia.* Swear not! if I must weep,
    Jove shall not smile at me;      50
This kiss, my heart, and thy faith keep!
*Cleon.* This breathes my soul to thee.

\* \* \* \*

Then forth the thicket Thyrsis rush'd,
    Where he saw all their play;
The swain stood still, and smiled, and blush'd:      55
    The nymph fled fast away.

GRIEF ENGROSSED.

Wherefore do thy sad numbers flow,
    So full of woe?
Why dost thou melt in such soft strains,
    Whilst she disdains?
    If she must still deny,     5
    Weep not, but die!
    And in thy funeral fire
    Shall all her fame expire.
Thus both shall perish, and as thou on thy hearse
Shall want her tears, so she shall want thy verse.  10
    Repine not then at thy blest state:
    Thou art above thy fate,
    But my fair Celia will not give
    Love enough to make me live;
    Nor yet dart from her eye     15
    Scorn enough to make me die.
Then let me weep alone till her kind breath
Or blow my tears away, or speak my death.

## A PASTORAL DIALOGUE.

### SHEPHERD, NYMPH, AND CHORUS.

*Shepherd.* THIS mossy bank they press'd. *Nymph.*
   That aged oak
  Did canopy the happy pair
  All night from the damp air.
*Chorus.* Here let us sit, and sing the words they
   spoke,
Till, the day breaking their embraces broke.    5
*Shepherd.* See, love, the blushes of the morn appear,
  And now she hangs her pearly store,
  Robb'd from the Eastern shore,
I' th' cowslip's bell and roses rare:
Sweet, I must stay no longer here.    10
*Nymph.* Those streaks of doubtful light usher not
   day,
  But show my sun must set; no morn
  Shall shine till thou return:
The yellow planets and the grey
Dawn shall attend thee on thy way.    15
*Shepherd.* If thine eyes gild my paths they may for-
   bear
  Their useless shine. *Nymph.* My tears will quite
  Extinguish their faint light.
*Shepherd.* Those drops will make their beams more
   clear,
Love's flames will shine in every tear.    20

*Chorus.* They kiss'd and wept, and from their lips
and eyes,
In a mix'd dew of briny sweet
Their joys and sorrows meet.
But she cries out. *Nymph.* Shepherd, arise!
The sun betrays us else to spies. 25

*Shepherd.* The winged hours fly fast whilst we
embrace;
But when we want their help to meet,
They move with leaden feet.
*Nymph.* Then let us pinion Time, and chase
The day for ever from this place. 30

*Shepherd.* Hark! *Nymph.* Ay me, stay! *Shepherd*
For ever! *Nymph.* No, arise!
We must be gone. *Shepherd.* My nest of spice!
*Nymph.* My soul! *Shepherd.* My Paradise!
*Chorus.* Neither could say farewell, but through their
eyes
Grief interrupted speech with tears' supplies. 35

### RED AND WHITE ROSES.

READ in these roses the sad story
Of my hard fate and your own glory.
  In the white you may discover
  The paleness of a fainting lover;
In the red the flames still feeding 5
On my heart, with fresh wounds bleeding.
  The white will tell you how I languish,
  And the red express my anguish;
The white my innocence displaying,
The red my martyrdom betraying. 10
  The frowns that on your brow resided,
  Have those roses thus divided.
Oh! let your smiles but clear the weather,
And then they both shall grow together.

## TO MY COUSIN (C. R.) MARRYING MY LADY (A.).

Happy youth! that shalt possess
  Such a spring-tide of delight,
    As the sated appetite
Shall, enjoying such excess,
Wish the flood of pleasure less;              5
    When the hymeneal rite
Is perform'd, invoke the night
That it may in shadows dress
Thy too real happiness:
    Else (as Semele) the bright            10
Deity, in her full might,
May thy feeble soul oppress.
  Strong perfumes and glaring light
  Oft destroy both smell and sight.

l. 5. The editions have *with the flood.*

## A LOVER,

### UPON AN ACCIDENT NECESSITATING HIS DEPARTURE, CONSULTS WITH REASON.

*Lover.*

Weep not, nor backward turn your beams,
   Fond eyes! Sad sighs, lock in your breath,
Lest on this wind, or in those streams,
   My grieved soul fly or sail to death.
Fortune destroys me if I stay,           5
Love kills me if I go away:
Since Love and Fortune both are blind,
Come, Reason, and resolve my doubtful mind.

*Reason.*

Fly! and blind Fortune be thy guide,
   And 'gainst the blinder god rebel.       10
Thy love-sick heart shall not reside
   Where scorn and self-will'd error dwell;
Where entrance unto Truth is barr'd,
Where Love and Faith find no reward:
For my just hand may sometimes move      15
The wheel of Fortune, not the sphere of Love.

## PARTING, CELIA WEEPS.

WEEP not, my dear, for I shall go
Laden enough with mine own woe;
Add not thy heaviness to mine;
Since fate our pleasures must disjoin,
Why should our sorrows meet? If I        5
Must go and lose thy company,
I wish not theirs: it shall relieve
My grief, to think thou dost not grieve.
Yet grieve and weep, that I may bear
Every sigh and every tear               10
Away with me; so shall thy breast
And eyes discharged enjoy their rest:
And it will glad my heart to see
Thou wert thus loth to part with me.

## A RAPTURE.

I WILL enjoy thee now, my Celia, come,
And fly with me to Love's Elysium.
The giant, Honour, that keeps cowards out,
Is but a masquer, and the servile rout
Of baser subjects only bend in vain          5
To the vast idol; whilst the nobler train
Of valiant lovers daily sail between
The huge Colossus' legs, and pass unseen
Unto the blissful shore. Be bold and wise,
And we shall enter: the grim Swiss denies    10
Only to tame fools a passage, that not know
He is but form and only frights in show
The duller eyes that look from far; draw near
And thou shalt scorn what we were wont to fear.
We shall see how the stalking pageant goes   15
With borrow'd legs, a heavy load to those
That made and bear him; not, as we once thought,
The seed of gods, but a weak model wrought
By greedy men, that seek to enclose the common,
And within private arms empale free woman.   20
   Come, then, and mounted on the wings of Love
We'll cut the flitting air and soar above
The monster's head, and in the noblest seats
Of those blest shades quench and renew our heats.
There shall the queens of love and innocence, 25
Beauty and Nature, banish all offence

From our close ivy-twines; there I'll behold
Thy bared snow and thy unbraided gold;
There my enfranchised hand on every side
Shall o'er thy naked polish'd ivory slide. 30
No curtain there, though of transparent lawn,
Shall be before thy virgin-treasure drawn;
But the rich mine, to the enquiring eye
Exposed, shall ready still for mintage lie,
And we will coin young Cupids. There a bed 35
Of roses and fresh myrtles shall be spread,
Under the cooler shade of cypress groves;
Our pillows of the down of Venus' doves,
Whereon our panting limbs we'll gently lay,
In the faint respites of our active play: 40
That so our slumbers may in dreams have leisure
To tell the nimble fancy our past pleasure,
And so our souls, that cannot be embraced,
Shall the embraces of our bodies taste.
Meanwhile the bubbling stream shall court the shore, 45
Th' enamour'd chirping wood-choir shall adore
In varied tunes the deity of love;
The gentle blasts of western winds shall move
The trembling leaves, and through their close boughs
    breathe
Still music, whilst we rest ourselves beneath 50
Their dancing shade; till a soft murmur, sent
From souls entranced in amorous languishment,
Rouse us, and shoot into our veins fresh fire,
Till we in their sweet ecstasy expire.
  Then, as the empty bee that lately bore 55
Into the common treasure all her store,

Flies 'bout the painted field with nimble wing,
Deflow'ring the fresh virgins of the spring,
So will I rifle all the sweets that dwell
In my delicious paradise, and swell                60
My bag with honey, drawn forth by the power
Of fervent kisses from each spicy flower.
I'll seize the rose-buds in their perfumed bed,
The violet knots, like curious mazes spread
O'er all the garden, taste the ripen'd cherry,    65
The warm firm apple, tipp'd with coral berry:
Then will I visit with a wand'ring kiss
The vale of lilies and the bower of bliss;
And where the beauteous region doth divide
Into two milky ways, my lips shall slide          70
Down those smooth alleys, wearing as they go
A tract for lovers on the printed snow;
Thence climbing o'er the swelling Apennine,
Retire into thy grove of eglantine,
Where I will all those ravish'd sweets distil     75
Through Love's alembic, and with chemic skill
From the mix'd mass one sovereign balm derive,
Then bring that great elixir to thy hive.
  Now in more subtle wreaths I will entwine
My sinewy thighs, my legs and arms with thine;    80
Thou like a sea of milk shalt lie display'd,
Whilst I the smooth calm ocean invade
With such a tempest, as when Jove of old
Fell down on Danaë in a storm of gold;
Yet my tall pine shall in the Cyprian strait      85
Ride safe at anchor and unlade her freight:
My rudder with thy bold hand, like a tried

And skilful pilot, thou shalt steer, and guide
My bark into love's channel, where it shall
Dance, as the bounding waves do rise or fall.  90
Then shall thy circling arms embrace and clip
My willing body, and thy balmy lip
Bathe me in juice of kisses, whose perfume
Like a religious incense shall consume,
And send up holy vapours to those powers  95
That bless our loves and crown our sportful hours,
That with such halcyon calmness fix our souls
In steadfast peace, as no affright controls.
There, no rude sounds shake us with sudden starts;
No jealous ears, when we unrip our hearts,  100
Suck our discourse in; no observing spies
This blush, that glance traduce; no envious eyes
Watch our close meetings; nor are we betray'd
To rivals by the bribed chambermaid.
No wedlock bonds unwreathe our twisted loves,  105
We seek no midnight arbour, no dark groves
To hide our kisses: there, the hated name
Of husband, wife, lust, modest, chaste or shame,
Are vain and empty words, whose very sound
Was never heard in the Elysian ground.  110
All things are lawful there, that may delight
Nature or unrestrained appetite;
Like and enjoy, to will and act is one:
We only sin when Love's rites are not done.

    The Roman Lucrece there reads the divine  115
Lectures of love's great master, Aretine,
And knows as well as Lais how to move
Her pliant body in the act of love;

To quench the burning ravisher she hurls
Her limbs into a thousand winding curls, 120
And studies artful postures, such as be
Carved on the bark of every neighbouring tree
By learned hands, that so adorn'd the rind
Of those fair plants, which, as they lay entwined,
Have fann'd their glowing fires. The Grecian
 dame, 125
That in her endless web toil'd for a name
As fruitless as her work, doth there display
Herself before the youth of Ithaca,
And th' amorous sport of gamesome nights prefer
Before dull dreams of the lost traveller. 130
Daphne hath broke her bark, and that swift foot
Which th' angry gods had fasten'd with a root
To the fix'd earth, doth now unfetter'd run
To meet th' embraces of the youthful Sun.
She hangs upon him like his Delphic lyre; 135
Her kisses blow the old, and breathe new fire;
Full of her god, she sings inspired lays,
Sweet odes of love, such as deserve the bays,
Which she herself was. Next her, Laura lies
In Petrarch's learned arms, drying those eyes 140
That did in such sweet smooth-paced numbers flow,
As made the world enamour'd of his woe.
These, and ten thousand beauties more, that died
Slave to the tyrant, now enlarged deride
His cancell'd laws, and for their time mis-spent 145
Pay into Love's exchequer double rent.

 Come then, my Celia, we'll no more forbear
To taste our joys, struck with a panic fear,

But will depose from his imperious sway
This proud usurper, and walk free as they, 150
With necks unyoked ; nor is it just that he
Should fetter your soft sex with chastity,
Whom Nature made unapt for abstinence ;
When yet this false impostor can dispense
With human justice and with sacred right, 155
And, maugre both their laws, command me fight
With rivals or with emulous loves that dare
Equal with thine their mistress' eyes or hair.
If thou complain of wrong, and call my sword
To carve out thy revenge, upon that word 160
He bids me fight and kill ; or else he brands
With marks of infamy my coward hands.
And yet religion bids from blood-shed fly,
And damns me for that act. Then tell me why
 This goblin Honour, which the world adores, 165
 Should make men atheists, and not women whores?

### EPITAPH ON THE LADY MARY VILLIERS.

The Lady Mary Villiers lies
Under this stone; with weeping eyes
The parents that first gave her birth,
And their sad friends, laid her in earth.
If any of them, Reader, were                5
Known unto thee, shed a tear;
Or if thyself possess a gem
As dear to thee, as this to them,
Though a stranger to this place,
Bewail in theirs thine own hard case:       10
For thou, perhaps, at thy return
Mayst find thy darling in an urn.

### ANOTHER.

The purest soul, that e'er was sent
Into a clayey tenement,
Inform'd this dust; but the weak mould
Could the great guest no longer hold:
The substance was too pure, the flame       5
Too glorious, that thither came.

Ten thousand Cupids brought along
A grace on each wing, that did throng
For place there, till they all oppress'd
The seat in which they sought to rest:   10
So the fair model broke, for want
Of room to lodge th' inhabitant.

### ANOTHER.

This little vault, this narrow room,
Of love and beauty is the tomb;
The dawning beam, that 'gan to clear
Our clouded sky, lies darken'd here,
For ever set to us, by death   5
Sent to inflame the world beneath.
'Twas but a bud, yet did contain
More sweetness than shall spring again;
A budding star, that might have grown
Into a sun when it had blown.   10
This hopeful beauty did create
New life in love's declining state;
But now his empire ends, and we
From fire and wounding darts are free;
His brand, his bow, let no man fear:   15
The flames, the arrows, all lie here.

### EPITAPH ON THE LADY S.

#### WIFE OF SIR W. S.

THE harmony of colours, features, grace,
Resulting airs (the magic of a face)
Of musical sweet tunes, all which combined
To crown one sovereign beauty, lies confined
To this dark vault. She was a cabinet 5
Where all the choicest stones of price were set:
Whose native colours and purest lustre lent
Her eye, cheek, lip, a dazzling ornament;
Whose rare and hidden virtues did express
Her inward beauties, and mind's fairer dress. 10
The constant diamond, the wise chrysolite,
The devout sapphire, emerald apt to write
Records of memory, cheerful agate, grave
And serious onyx, topaz that doth save
The brain's calm temper, witty amethyst, 15
This precious quarry, or what else the list
On Aaron's ephod planted had, she wore:
One only pearl was wanting to her store,
Which in her Saviour's book she found express'd:
To purchase that, she sold Death all the rest. 20

## MARIA WENTWORTH,

### THOMÆ COMITIS CLEVELAND FILIA PRÆMORTUÆ PRIMA VIRGINEAM ANIMAM EXHALUIT: ANNO DOMINI ———. ÆTATIS SUÆ ———.

AND here the precious dust is laid,
Whose purely-temper'd clay was made
So fine, that it the guest betray'd.

Else, the soul grew so fast within
It broke the outward shell of sin,  5
And so was hatch'd a Cherubin.

In height it soar'd to God above;
In depth it did to knowledge move,
And spread in breadth to general love.

Before, a pious duty shined  10
To parents; courtesy behind;
On either side, an equal mind.

Good to the poor, to kindred dear,
To servants kind, to friendship clear:
To nothing but herself severe.  15

So, though a virgin, yet a bride
To every grace, she justified
A chaste polygamy, and died.

Learn from hence, Reader, what small trust
We owe this world, where virtue must,  20
Frail as our flesh, crumble to dust.

## ON THE DUKE OF BUCKINGHAM.

BEATISSIMIS MANIBUS CARISSIMI VIRI ILLUSTRIS-
SIMA CONJUX SIC PARENTAVIT.

WHEN in the brazen leaves of Fame
The life, the death of Buckingham
Shall be recorded, if Truth's hand
Incise the story of our land,
Posterity shall see a fair 5
Structure, by the studious care
Of two kings raised, that no less
Their wisdom than their power express.
By blinded zeal, (whose doubtful light
Made murder's scarlet robe seem white; 10
Whose vain-deluding phantoms charm'd
A clouded sullen soul, and arm'd
A desperate hand, thirsty of blood,)
Torn from the fair earth where it stood,
So the majestic fabric fell. 15
His actions let our annals tell;
We write no chronicle; this pile
Wears only sorrow's face and style,
Which even the envy that did wait
Upon his flourishing estate, 20
Turn'd to soft pity of his death,
Now pays his hearse: but that cheap breath

Shall not blow here, nor th' unpure brine
Puddle those streams that bathe this shrine.
   These are the pious obsequies          25
Dropp'd from his chaste wife's pregnant eyes
In frequent showers, and were alone
By her congealing sighs made stone,
On which the carver did bestow
These forms and characters of woe:         30
So he the fashion only lent,
Whilst she wept all this monument.


### ANOTHER.

SISTE, HOSPES, SIVE INDIGENA, SIVE ADVENA, VICISSITUDINIS RERUM MEMOR, PAUCA PELLEGE.

READER, when these dumb stones have told
In borrow'd speech what guest they hold
Thou shalt confess the vain pursuit
Of human glory yields no fruit
But an untimely grave.   If Fate            5
Could constant happiness create,
Her ministers, Fortune and Worth,
Had here that miracle brought forth:
They fix'd this child of Honour where
No room was left for hope or fear,          10
Of more or less; so high, so great
His growth was, yet so safe his seat.
Safe in the circle of his friends,
Safe in his loyal heart, and ends;

Safe in his native valiant spirit, 15
By favour safe, and safe by merit;
Safe by the stamp of Nature, which
Did strength with shape and grace enrich;
Safe in the cheerful courtesies
Of flowing gestures, speech, and eyes; 20
Safe in his bounties, which were more
Proportion'd to his mind than store:
Yet, though for virtue he becomes
Involved himself in borrow'd sums,
Safe in his care, he leaves betray'd 25
No friend engaged, no debt unpaid.
    But though the stars conspire to shower
Upon one head th' united power
Of all their graces, if their dire
Aspects must other breasts inspire 30
With vicious thoughts, a murderer's knife
May cut, as here, their darling's life.
Who can be happy then, if Nature must
To make one happy man, make all men just?

# FOUR SONGS, BY WAY OF CHORUS TO A PLAY.

### AT AN ENTERTAINMENT OF THE KING AND QUEEN, BY MY LORD CHAMBERLAIN.

#### THE FIRST OF JEALOUSY. DIALOGUE.

*Question.* FROM whence was first this fury hurl'd,
This jealousy, into the world?
Came she from hell? *Answer.* No, there doth reign
Eternal hatred, with disdain;
But she the daughter is of Love,                      5
Sister of Beauty. *Question.* Then above
She must derive from the third sphere
Her heavenly offspring? *Answer.* Neither there,
From those immortal flames, could she
Draw her cold frozen pedigree.                       10
*Question.* If nor from heaven nor hell, where then
Had she her birth? *Answer.* I' th' hearts of men.
Beauty and Fear did her create,
Younger than Love, elder than Hate,
Sister to both; by Beauty's side                     15
To Love, by Fear to Hate, allied.
Despair her issue is, whose race
Of fruitful mischiefs drowns the space
Of the wide earth in a swoln flood
Of wrath, revenge, spite, rage, and blood.           20

l. 6. *Question.* The printed copies have here *Reply*.

*Question.* Oh, how can such a spurious line
Proceed from parents so divine?
*Answer.* As streams which from their crystal spring
Do sweet and clear their waters bring,
Yet, mingling with the brackish main, 25
Nor taste nor colour they retain.
*Question.* Yet rivers 'twixt their own banks flow
Still fresh; can Jealousy do so?
*Answer.* Yes, whilst she keeps the steadfast ground
Of Hope and Fear, her equal bound. 30
Hope sprung from favour, worth, or chance,
Towards the fair object doth advance;
Whilst Fear, as watchful sentinel,
Doth the invading foe repel:
And Jealousy, thus mix'd, doth prove 35
The season and the salt of love.
But when Fear takes a larger scope,
Stifling the child of Reason, Hope,
Then, sitting on th' usurped throne,
She like a tyrant rules alone: 40
As the wild ocean unconfined,
And raging as the northern wind.

II.

### FEMININE HONOUR.

In what esteem did the gods hold
    Fair innocence and the chaste bed,
When scandal'd Virtue might be bold
    Bare-foot upon sharp culters, spread
O'er burning coals, to march; yet feel    5
Nor scorching fire nor piercing steel?

Why, when the hard-edged iron did turn
    Soft as a bed of roses blown,
When cruel flames forgot to burn
    Their chaste pure limbs, should man alone  10
'Gainst female innocence conspire
Harder than steel, fiercer than fire?

Oh, hapless sex! Unequal sway
    Of partial honour! Who may know
Rebels from subjects that obey,    15
    When malice can on vestals throw
Disgrace, and fame fix high repute
On the close shameless prostitute?

Vain Honour! thou art but disguise,
    A cheating voice, a juggling art;    20
No judge of virtue, whose pure eyes
    Court her own image in the heart,
More pleased with her true figure there
Than her false echo in the ear.

### III.

#### SEPARATION OF LOVERS.

Stop the chafed boar, or play
  With the lion's paw, yet fear
  From the lover's side to tear
The idol of his soul away.

Though love enter by the sight    5
  To the heart, it doth not fly
  From the mind, when from the eye
The fair objects take their flight.

But since want provokes desire,
  When we lose what we before    10
  Have enjoy'd, as we want more,
So is love more set on fire.

Love doth with an hungry eye
  Glut on beauty; and you may
  Safer snatch the tiger's prey,    15
Than his vital food deny.

Yet though absence for a space
  Sharpen the keen appetite,
  Long continuance doth quite
All love's characters efface:    20

For the sense, not fed, denies
  Nourishment unto the mind,
  Which with expectation pined,
Love of a consumption dies.

## IV.

### INCOMMUNICABILITY OF LOVE.

*Question.* By what power was love confined
  To one object? Who can bind,
Or fix a limit to the free-born mind?

*Answer.* Nature: for as bodies may
  Move at once but in one way,    5
So nor can minds to more than one love stray.

*Question.* Yet I feel a double smart,
  Love's twinn'd flame, his forked dart.
*Answer.* Then hath wild lust, not love, possess'd
  thy heart.

*Question.* Whence springs love? *Ans.* From
  beauty. *Question.* Why    10
  Should th' effect not multiply
As fast i' th' heart, as doth the cause i' th' eye?

*Answer.* When two beauties equal are,
  Sense preferring neither fair,
Desire stands still, distracted 'twixt the pair.    15

So in equal distance lay
  Two fair lambs in the wolf's way,
The hungry beast will starve ere choose his prey.

But where one is chief, the rest
  Cease, and that's alone possess'd,    20
Without a rival, monarch of the breast.

### SONGS IN THE PLAY.

#### A LOVER, IN THE DISGUISE OF AN AMAZON, IS DEARLY BELOVED OF HIS MISTRESS.

CEASE, thou afflicted soul, to mourn,
Whose love and faith are paid with scorn;
For I am starved that feel the blisses
Of dear embraces, smiles, and kisses
From my soul's idol, yet complain      5
Of equal love more than disdain.

Cease, beauty's exile, to lament
The frozen shades of banishment;
For I in that fair bosom dwell,
That is my paradise and hell:      10
Banish'd at home, at once at ease
In the safe port and toss'd on seas.

Cease in cold jealous fears to pine,
Sad wretch, whom rivals undermine;
For though I hold lock'd in mine arms      15
My life's sole joy, a traitor's charms
Prevail: whilst I may only blame
Myself, that mine own rival am.

### ANOTHER.

A LADY, RESCUED FROM DEATH BY A KNIGHT, WHO IN THE INSTANT LEAVES HER, COMPLAINS THUS:

OH, whither is my fair sun fled
   Bearing his light, not heat, away?
If thou repose in the moist bed
   Of the Sea-Queen, bring back the day
To our dark clime, and thou shalt lie     5
Bathed in the sea flows from mine eye.

Upon what whirlwind didst thou ride
   Hence, yet remain fix'd in my heart,
From me and to me fled and tied?
   Dark riddles of the amorous art!     10
Love lent thee wings to fly, so he
Unfeather'd now must rest with me.

Help, help, brave youth! I burn, I bleed!
   The cruel god with bow and brand
Pursues the life thy valour freed;     15
   Disarm him with thy conquering hand,
And that thou mayst the wild boy tame,
Give me his dart, keep thou his flame.

## TO BEN JONSON.

### UPON OCCASION OF HIS ODE OF DEFIANCE ANNEXED TO HIS PLAY OF THE NEW INN.

'TIS true, dear Ben, thy just chastizing hand
Hath fix'd upon the sotted age a brand,
To their swoln pride and empty scribbling due;
It can nor judge nor write: and yet 'tis true
Thy comic Muse, from the exalted line 5
Touch'd by thy *Alchymist*, doth since decline
From that her zenith, and foretells a red
And blushing evening, when she goes to bed;
Yet such as shall outshine the glimmering light
With which all stars shall gild the following night; 10
Nor think it much, since all thy eaglets may
Endure the sunny trial, if we say
This hath the stronger wing, or, that doth shine
Trick'd up in fairer plumes, since all are thine.
Who hath his flock of cackling geese compared 15
With thy tuned choir of swans? or else who dared
To call thy births deform'd? but if thou bind
By city-custom or by gavel-kind
In equal shares thy love on all thy race,
We may distinguish of their sex and place; 20
Though one hand form them, and though one brain strike
Souls into all, they are not all alike.
Why should the follies, then, of this dull age

Draw from thy pen such an immodest rage,
As seems to blast thy else-immortal bays,   25
When thine own tongue proclaims thy itch of praise?
Such thirst will argue drought.   No, let be hurl'd
Upon thy works by the detracting world
What malice can suggest: let the rout say,
The running sands that ere thou make a play   30
Count the slow minutes, might a Goodwin frame,
To swallow when th' hast done thy shipwreck'd
    name.
Let them the dear expense of oil upbraid,
Suck'd by thy watchful lamp, that hath betray'd
To theft the blood of martyr'd authors, spilt   35
Into thy ink, whilst thou growest pale with guilt.
Repine not at the taper's thrifty waste,
That sleeks thy terser poems ; nor is haste
Praise, but excuse ; and if thou overcome
A knotty writer, bring the booty home ;   40
Nor think it theft, if the rich spoils so torn
From conquer'd authors be as trophies worn.
Let others glut on the extorted praise
Of vulgar breath ; trust thou to after days :
Thy labour'd works shall live, when Time devours 45
Th' abortive offspring of their hasty hours.
Thou art not of their rank, the quarrel lies
Within thine own verge: then let this suffice,
The wiser world doth greater thee confess
Than all men else, than thyself only less.   50

## AN HYMENEAL DIALOGUE.

### BRIDE AND GROOM.

*Groom.*

TELL me, my love, since Hymen tied
    The holy knot, hast thou not felt
A new infused spirit slide
    Into thy breast, whilst thine did melt?

*Bride.*

First tell me, sweet, whose words were those? 5
    For though your voice the air did break,
Yet did my soul the sense compose,
    And through your lips my heart did speak.

*Groom.*

Then I perceive, when from the flame
    Of love my scorch'd soul did retire, 10
Your frozen heart in her place came,
    And sweetly melted in that fire.

*Bride.*

'Tis true, for when that mutual change
    Of souls was made, with equal gain,
I straight might feel diffused a strange 15
    But gentle heat through every vein.

l. 6. The 1640 edition has For though the voice your air did break.

*Chorus.*

O blest disunion ! that doth so
  Our bodies from our souls divide,
As two do one, and one four grow,
  Each by contraction multiplied.     20

*Bride.*

Thy bosom then I'll make my nest,
  Since there my willing soul doth perch.
*Groom.* And for my heart in thy chaste breast,
  I'll make an everlasting search.

*Chorus.*

O blest disunion ! that doth so     25
  Our bodies from our souls divide,
As two do one, and one four grow,
  Each by contraction multiplied.

## OBSEQUIES TO THE LADY ANNE HAY.

I HEARD the virgins sigh, I saw the sleek
And polish'd courtier channel his fresh cheek
With real tears; the new-betrothed maid
Smiled not that day; the graver senate laid
Their business by: of all the courtly throng        5
Grief seal'd the heart, and silence bound the tongue.
I, that ne'er more of private sorrow knew
Than from my pen some froward mistress drew,
And for the public woe had my dull sense
So sear'd with ever-adverse influence,                10
As the invader's sword might have, unfelt,
Pierced my dead bosom, yet began to melt:
Grief's strong instinct did to my blood suggest
In the unknown loss peculiar interest.
But when I heard the noble Carlisle's gem,            15
The fairest branch of Denny's ancient stem,
Was from that casket stol'n, from this trunk torn,
I found just cause why they, why I, should mourn.
  But who shall guide my artless pen to draw
Those blooming beauties, which I never saw?           20
How shall posterity believe my story,

If I her crowded graces, and the glory
Due to her riper virtues, shall relate
Without the knowledge of her mortal state?
Shall I (as once Apelles), here a feature, 25
There steal a grace, and rifling so whole Nature
Of all the sweets a learned eye can see,
Figure one Venus, and say, Such was she?
Shall I her legend fill, with what of old
Hath of the worthies of her sex been told; 30
And what all pens and times to all dispense,
Restrain to her, by a prophetic sense?
Or shall I to the moral and divine
Exactest laws shape, by an even line,
A life so straight, as it should shame the square 35
Left in the rules of Catherine or Clare,
And call it hers? say, So did she begin,
And, had she lived, such had her progress been.
These are dull ways, by which base pens for hire
Daub glorious vice, and from Apollo's choir 40
Steal holy ditties, which profanely they
Upon the hearse of every strumpet lay.
We will not bathe thy corpse with a forced tear,
Nor shall thy train borrow the blacks they wear;
Such vulgar spice and gums embalm not thee, 45
Thou art the theme of truth, not poetry.
Thou shalt endure a trial by thy peers;
Virgins of equal birth, of equal years,
Whose virtues held with thine an emulous strife,
Shall draw thy picture, and record thy life. 50
One shall ensphere thine eyes; another shall
Impearl thy teeth; a third, thy white and small

Hand shall besnow; a fourth, incarnadine
Thy rosy cheek: until each beauteous line,
Drawn by her hand in whom that part excels,   55
Meets in one centre, where all beauty dwells.
   Others, in task, shall thy choice virtues share,
Some shall their birth, some their ripe growth
    declare;
Though niggard Time left much unhatch'd by deeds,
They shall relate how thou hadst all the seeds   60
Of every virtue, which, in the pursuit
Of time, must have brought forth admired fruit.
Thus shalt thou, from the mouth of envy, raise
A glorious journal of thy thrifty days:
Like a bright star shot from his sphere, whose
    race   65
In a continued line of flames we trace.
This, if survey'd, shall to thy view impart
How little more than late thou wert, thou art.
This shall gain credit with succeeding times,
When, nor by bribed pens, nor partial rhymes   70
Of engaged kindred, but the sacred truth
Is storied by the partners of thy youth:
Their breath shall saint thee, and be this thy pride
Thus even by rivals to be deified.

## TO THE COUNTESS OF ANGLESEY.

### UPON THE IMMODERATELY-BY-HER-LAMENTED DEATH OF HER HUSBAND.

MADAM, men say you keep with dropping eyes
Your sorrows fresh, wat'ring the rose, that lies
Fall'n from your cheeks, upon your dear lord's hearse.
Alas! those odours now no more can pierce
His cold pale nostril, nor the crimson dye           5
Present a graceful blush to his dark eye.
Think you that flood of pearly moisture hath
The virtue fabled of old Æson's bath?
You may your beauties and your youth consume
Over his urn, and with your sighs perfume           10
The solitary vault, which, as you groan,
In hollow echoes shall repeat your moan;
There you may wither, and an autumn bring
Upon yourself, but not call back his spring.
Forbear your fruitless grief, then, and let those    15
Whose love was doubted, gain belief with shows
To their suspected faith. You, whose whole life
In every act crown'd you a constant wife,
May spare the practice of that vulgar trade,
Which superstitious custom only made.                20
Rather, a widow now, of wisdom prove
The pattern, as, a wife, you were of love.
Yet since you surfeit on your grief, 'tis fit
I tell the world upon what cates you sit
Glutting your sorrows; and at once include           25
His story, your excuse, my gratitude.

You, that behold how yond sad lady blends
Those ashes with her tears, lest, as she spends
Her tributary sighs, the frequent gust
Might scatter up and down the noble dust,    30
Know, when that heap of atoms was with blood
Kneaded to solid flesh, and firmly stood
On stately pillars, the rare form might move
The froward Juno's or chaste Cinthia's love.
In motion, active grace, in rest, a calm    35
Attractive sweetness, brought both wound and balm
To every heart. He was composed of all
The wishes of ripe virgins, when they call
For Hymen's rites, and in their fancies wed
A shape of studied beauties to their bed.    40
Within this curious palace dwelt a soul
Gave lustre to each part, and to the whole:
This dress'd his face in courteous smiles, and so
From comely gestures sweeter manners flow;
This courage join'd to strength; so the hand,
    bent,    45
Was valour's, open'd, bounty's instrument,
Which did the scale and sword of Justice hold,
Knew how to brandish steel and scatter gold.
This taught him, not to engage his modest tongue
In suits of private gain, though public wrong;    50
Nor misemploy (as is the great man's use,)
His credit with his master to traduce,
Deprave, malign, and ruin innocence,
In proud revenge of some mis-judged offence:
But all his actions had the noble end    55
T' advance desert, or grace some worthy friend.

He chose not in the active stream to swim,
Nor hunted Honour, which yet hunted him;
But like a quiet eddy, that hath found
Some hollow creek, there turns his waters round,  60
And in continual circles dances free
From the impetuous torrent; so did he
Give others leave to turn the wheel of State,
(Whose restless motion spins the subjects' fate,)
Whilst he, retired from the tumultuous noise  65
Of Court, and suitors' press, apart enjoys
Freedom and mirth, himself, his time, and friends,
And with sweet relish tastes each hour he spends.

  I could remember how his noble heart
First kindled at your beauties; with what art  70
He chased his game through all opposing fears,
When I his sighs to you, and back your tears
Convey'd to him; how loyal then, and how
Constant he proved since to his marriage-vow;
So as his wand'ring eyes never drew in  75
One lustful thought to tempt his soul to sin:
But that I fear such mention rather may
Kindle new grief, than blow the old away.

  Then let him rest, join'd to great Buckingham,
And with his brother's mingle his bright flame.  80
Look up and meet their beams, and you from thence
May chance derive a cheerful influence.
Seek him no more in dust, but call agen
Your scatter'd beauties home; and so the pen,
Which now I take from this sad elegy,  85
Shall sing the trophies of your conquering eye.

    l. 64. The original edition has *motions*.

## AN ELEGY UPON THE DEATH OF DR. DONNE, DEAN OF PAUL'S.

Can we not force from widow'd poetry,
Now thou art dead, great Donne, one elegy,
To crown thy hearse?  Why yet did we not trust,
Though with unkneaded dough-baked prose, thy dust,
Such as the unscissor'd lecturer, from the flower   5
Of fading rhetoric, short-lived as his hour,
Dry as the sand that measures it, might lay
Upon the ashes on the funeral day?
Have we nor tune nor voice?  Didst thou dispense
Through all our language both the words and sense?   10
'Tis a sad truth.  The pulpit may her plain
And sober Christian precepts still retain;
Doctrines it may, and wholesome uses, frame,
Grave homilies and lectures; but the flame
Of thy brave soul, that shot such heat and light,   15
As burn'd our earth, and made our darkness bright,
Committed holy rapes upon the will,
Did through the eye the melting heart distil,
And the deep knowledge of dark truths so teach,
As sense might judge what fancy could not reach,   20

Must be desired for ever.  So the fire,
That fills with spirit and heat the Delphic choir,
Which, kindled first by thy Promethean breath,
Glow'd here awhile, lies quench'd now in thy death.
The Muses' garden, with pedantic weeds        25
O'erspread, was purged by thee; the lazy seeds
Of servile imitation thrown away,
And fresh invention planted; thou didst pay
The debts of our penurious bankrupt age;
Licentious thefts, that make poetic rage        30
A mimic fury, when our souls must be
Possess'd, or with Anacreon's ecstasy,
Or Pindar's, not their own; the subtle cheat
Of sly exchanges, and the juggling feat
Of two-edged words, or whatsoever wrong        35
By ours was done the Greek or Latin tongue,
Thou hast redeem'd, and open'd us a mine
Of rich and pregnant fancy; drawn a line
Of masculine expression, which, had good
Old Orpheus seen, or all the ancient brood        40
Our superstitious fools admire, and hold
Their lead more precious than thy burnish'd gold,
Thou hadst been their exchequer, and no more
They each in other's dung had search'd for ore.
Thou shalt yield no precedence, but of time,        45
And the blind fate of language, whose tuned chime
More charms the outward sense: yet thou mayst claim
From so great disadvantage greater fame,
Since to the awe of thy imperious wit
Our troublesome language bends, made only fit        50

With her tough thick-ribb'd hoops to gird about
Thy giant fancy, which had proved too stout
For their soft melting phrases. As in time
They had the start, so did they cull the prime
Buds of invention many a hundred year,     55
And left the rifled fields, besides the fear
To touch their harvest; yet from those bare lands,
Of what was only thine, thy only hands
(And that their smallest work,) have gleaned more
Than all those times and tongues could reap
 before.     60

 But thou art gone, and thy strict laws will be
Too hard for libertines in poetry;
They will recall the goodly exiled train
Of gods and goddesses, which in thy just reign
Was banish'd nobler poems; now with these,     65
The silenced tales i' th' Metamorphoses,
Shall stuff their lines, and swell the windy page,
Till verse, refined by thee in this last age,
Turn ballad-rhyme, or those old idols be
Adored again with new apostacy.     70

 O pardon me, that break with untuned verse
The reverend silence that attends thy hearse,
Whose solemn awful murmurs were to thee,
More than these rude lines, a loud elegy,
That did proclaim in a dumb eloquence     75
The death of all the arts: whose influence,
Grown feeble, in these panting numbers lies,
Gasping short-winded accents, and so dies.
So doth the swiftly-turning wheel not stand
In th' instant we withdraw the moving hand,     80

But some short time retain a faint weak course,
By virtue of the first impulsive force:
And so, whilst I cast on thy funeral pile
Thy crown of bays, oh let it crack awhile,
And spit disdain, till the devouring flashes        85
Suck all the moisture up, then turn to ashes.
  I will not draw the envy to engross
All thy perfections, or weep all the loss;
Those are too numerous for one elegy,
And this too great to be express'd by me.           90
Let others carve the rest; it shall suffice
I on thy grave this epitaph incise:—

    *Here lies a king that ruled, as he thought fit,*
    *The universal monarchy of wit;*
    *Here lies two flamens, and both those the best:*  95
    *Apollo's first, at last the true God's priest.*

IN ANSWER OF AN ELEGIACAL LETTER, UPON THE DEATH OF THE KING OF SWEDEN FROM AURELIAN TOWNSEND, INVITING ME TO WRITE ON THAT SUBJECT.

WHY dost thou sound, my dear Aurelian,
In so shrill accents from thy Barbican
A loud alarum to my drowsy eyes,
Bidding them wake in tears and elegies
For mighty Sweden's fall? Alas! how may      5
My lyric feet, that of the smooth soft way
Of love and beauty only know the tread
In dancing paces, celebrate the dead
Victorious king, or his majestic hearse
Profane with th' humble touch of their low verse?   10
Virgil, nor Lucan, no, nor Tasso, more
Than both, not Donne, worth all that went before,
With the united labour of their wit,
Could a just poem to this subject fit.
His actions were too mighty to be raised      15
Higher by verse: let him in prose be praised,
In modest faithful story, which his deeds
Shall turn to poems. When the next age reads
Of Frankfort, Leipzig, Wurzburg, of the Rhine,
The Lech, the Danube, Tilly, Wallenstein,      20
Bavaria, Pappenheim, Lutzen-field, where he
Gain'd after death a posthume victory,

They'll think his acts things rather feign'd than done,
Like our romances of The Knight o' th' Sun.
Leave we him, then, to the grave chronicler,     25
Who, though to annals he cannot refer
His too-brief story, yet his journals may
Stand by the Cæsars' years, and, every day
Cut into minutes, each shall more contain
Of great designment than an emperor's reign.     30
And, since 'twas but his church-yard, let him have
For his own ashes now no narrower grave
Than the whole German continent's vast womb,
Whilst all her cities do but make his tomb.
Let us to supreme Providence commit     35
The fate of monarchs, which first thought it fit
To rend the empire from the Austrian grasp;
And next from Sweden's, even when he did clasp
Within his dying arms the sovereignty
Of all those provinces, that men might see     40
The Divine wisdom would not leave that land
Subject to any one king's sole command.
Then let the Germans fear, if Cæsar shall,
Or the united princes, rise and fall;
But let us, that in myrtle bowers sit     45
Under secure shades, use the benefit
Of peace and plenty, which the blessed hand
Of our good king gives this obdurate land;
Let us of revels sing, and let thy breath,
(Which filled Fame's trumpet with Gustavus' death,
Blowing his name to heaven), gently inspire     51
Thy pastoral pipe, till all our swains admire
Thy song and subject, whilst they both comprise

The beauties of the SHEPHERD'S PARADISE.
For who like thee (whose loose discourse is far 55
More neat and polish'd than our poems are,
Whose very gait's more graceful than our dance)
In sweetly-flowing numbers may advance
The glorious night when, not to act foul rapes
Like birds or beasts, but in their angel shapes, 60
A troop of deities came down to guide
Our steerless barks in passion's swelling tide
By virtue's card, and brought us from above
A pattern of their own celestial love;
Nor lay it in dark sullen precepts drown'd, 65
But with rich fancy and clear action crown'd,
Through a mysterious fable (that was drawn,
Like a transparent veil of purest lawn,
Before their dazzling beauties) the divine
Venus did with her heavenly Cupid shine. 70
The story's curious web, the masculine style,
The subtle sense, did time and sleep beguile;
Pinion'd and charm'd they stood, to gaze upon
Th' angel-like forms, gestures and motion;
To hear those ravishing sounds, that did dispense 75
Knowledge and pleasure to the soul and sense.
It fill'd us with amazement to behold
Love made all spirit; his corporeal mould
Dissected into atoms, melt away
To empty air, and, from the gross allay 80
Of mixtures and compounding accidents,
Refined to immaterial elements.
But when the Queen of Beauty did inspire
The air with perfumes, and our hearts with fire,

Breathing from her celestial organ sweet 85
Harmonious notes, our souls fell at her feet,
And did with humble reverend duty more
Her rare perfections than high state adore.
   These harmless pastimes let my Townsend sing
To rural tunes; not that thy Muse wants wing 90
To soar a loftier pitch, for she hath made
A noble flight, and placed th' heroic shade
Above the reach of our faint flagging rhyme;
But these are subjects proper to our clime,
Tourneys, masques, theatres, better become 95
Our halcyon days. What though the German drum
Bellow for freedom and revenge, the noise
Concerns not us, nor should divert our joys;
Nor ought the thunder of their carabines
Drown the sweet airs of our tuned violins. 100
Believe me, friend, if their prevailing powers
Gain them a calm security like ours,
They'll hang their arms upon the olive bough,
And dance and revel then, as we do now.

## UPON MASTER W. MONTAGUE, HIS RETURN FROM TRAVEL.

Lead the black bull to slaughter, with the boar
And lamb; then purple with their mingled gore
The ocean's curled brow, that so we may
The sea-gods for their careful waftage pay:
Send grateful incense up in pious smoke          5
To those mild spirits, that cast a curbing yoke
Upon the stubborn winds, that calmly blew
To the wish'd shore our long'd-for Montague.
Then, whilst the aromatic odours burn
In honour of their darling's safe return,        10
The Muses' choir shall thus with voice and hand
Bless the fair gale that drove his ship to land:

*Sweetly breathing vernal air,*
*That with kind warmth dost repair*
*Winter's ruins; from whose breast*              15
*All the gums and spice of th' East*
*Borrow their perfumes; whose eye*
*Gilds the morn and clears the sky;*
*Whose dishevell'd tresses shed*
*Pearls upon the violet bed;*                    20
*On whose brow, with calm smiles dress'd,*
*The halcyon sits and builds her nest;*
*Beauty, youth, and endless spring*

Dwell upon thy rosy wing.
Thou, if stormy Boreas' throws       25
Down whole forests when he blows,
With a pregnant flowery birth
Canst refresh the teeming earth;
If he nip the early bud,
If he blast what's fair or good,     30
If he scatter our choice flowers,
If he shake our hills or bowers,
If his rude breath threaten us,
Thou canst stroke great Æolus,
And from him the grace obtain        35
To bind him in an iron chain.

Thus, whilst you deal your body 'mongst your friends,
And fill their circling arms, my glad soul sends
This, her embrace: thus we of Delphos greet;
As laymen clasp their hands, we join our feet.   40

### TO MASTER W. MONTAGUE.

SIR, I arrest you at your country's suit,
Who, as a debt to her, requires the fruit
Of that rich stock, which she by Nature's hand
Gave you in trust, to th' use of this whole land.
Next, she indicts you of a felony,               5
For stealing what was her propriety,
Yourself, from hence: so seeking to convey

The public treasure of the State away.
More, you're accused of ostracism, the fate
Imposed of old by the Athenian state          10
On eminent virtue; but that curse, which they
Cast on their men, you on your country lay.
For, thus divided from your noble parts,
This kingdom lives in exile, and all hearts
That relish worth or honour, being rent       15
From your perfections, suffer banishment.
These are your public injuries; but I
Have a just private quarrel to defy,
And call you coward, thus to run away
When you had pierced my heart, not daring stay 20
Till I redeem'd my honour: but I swear
By Celia's eyes, by the same force to tear
Your heart from you, or not to end this strife
Till I or find revenge or lose my life.
But as in single fights it oft hath been       25
In that unequal equal trial seen,
That he who had received the wrong at first
Came from the combat oft too with the worst;
So, if you foil me when we meet, I'll then
Give you fair leave to wound me so agen.       30

## ON THE MARRIAGE OF T. K. AND C. C.; THE MORNING STORMY.

Such should this day be, so the sun should hide
His bashful face, and let the conquering bride
Without a rival shine, whilst he forbears
To mingle his unequal beams with hers;
Or if sometimes he glance his squinting eye  5
Between the parting clouds, 'tis but to spy,
Not emulate, her glories; so comes dress'd
In veils, but as a masquer to the feast.
Thus heaven should lower, such stormy gusts should
    blow,
Not to denounce ungentle fates, but show  10
The cheerful bridegroom to the clouds and wind
Hath all his tears and all his sighs assign'd.
Let tempests struggle in the air, but rest
Eternal calms within thy peaceful breast,
Thrice happy youth! but ever sacrifice  15
To that fair hand that dried thy blubber'd eyes,
That crown'd thy head with roses, and turn'd all
The plagues of love into a cordial,
When first it join'd her virgin snow to thine;
Which, when to-day the priest shall re-combine,  20
From the mysterious holy touch such charms
Will flow, as shall unlock her wreathed arms,
And open a free passage to that fruit
Which thou hast toil'd for with a long pursuit.
But ere thou feed, that thou mayst better taste  25
Thy present joys, think on thy torments past;
Think on the mercy freed thee; think upon

Her virtues, graces, beauties, one by one:
So shalt thou relish all, enjoy the whole
Delights of her fair body and pure soul.　　　30
Then boldly to the fight of love proceed!
'Tis mercy not to pity, though she bleed.
We'll strew no nuts, but change that ancient form,
For till to-morrow we'll prorogue this storm;
Which shall confound, with its loud whistling noise, 35
Her pleasing shrieks, and fan thy panting joys.


### FOR A PICTURE, WHERE A QUEEN LAMENTS OVER THE TOMB OF A SLAIN KNIGHT.

BRAVE youth, to whom Fate in one hour
Gave death and conquest, by whose power
Those chains about my heart are wound,
With which the foe my kingdom bound:
Freed and captived by thee, I bring　　　5
For either act an offering.
For victory, this wreath of bay;
In sign of thraldom, down I lay
Sceptre and crown; take from my sight
Those royal robes; since Fortune's spite　　　10
Forbids me live thy virtue's prize,
I'll die thy valour's sacrifice.

## TO A LADY, THAT DESIRED I WOULD LOVE HER.

### I.

Now you have freely given me leave to love,
          What will you do?
Shall I your mirth or passion move
          When I begin to woo?
Will you torment, or scorn, or love me too?     5

### II.

Each petty beauty can disdain, and I,
          Spite of your hate,
Without your leave can see, and die.
          Dispense a nobler fate!
'Tis easy to destroy: you may create.     10

### III.

Then give me leave to love, and love me too:
          Not with design
To raise, as Love's curst rebels do,
          When puling poets whine,
Fame to their beauty, from their blubber'd eyne.     15

### IV.

Grief is a puddle, and reflects not clear
          Your beauty's rays;

Joys are pure streams; your eyes appear
    Sullen in sadder lays;
In cheerful numbers they shine bright with praise, 20

### V.

Which shall not mention, to express you fair,
    Wounds, flames, and darts,
Storms in your brow, nets in your hair,
    Suborning all your parts,
Or to betray, or torture captive hearts.    25

### VI.

I'll make your eyes like morning suns appear,
    As mild and fair;
Your brow as crystal smooth and clear;
    And your dishevell'd hair
Shall flow like a calm region of the air.    30

### VII.

Rich Nature's store, which is the poet's treasure,
    I'll spend to dress
Your beauties, if your mine of pleasure
    In equal thankfulness
You but unlock, so we each other bless.    35

UPON MY LORD CHIEF JUSTICE
HIS ELECTION OF MY LADY A. W.
FOR HIS MISTRESS.

I

    HEAR this, and tremble, all
Usurping Beauties, that create
A government tyrannical,
    In Love's free state !
Justice hath to the sword of your edged eyes    5
His equal balance join'd ; his sage head lies
In Love's soft lap, which must be just and wise.

II.

    Hark ! how the stern law breathes
Forth amorous sighs, and now prepares
No fetters, but of silken wreaths,    10
    And braided hairs ;
His dreadful rods and axes are exiled,
Whilst he sits crown'd with roses : Love hath filed
His native roughness ; Justice is grown mild.

III.

    The golden age returns !    15
Love's bow and quiver useless lie ;

His shaft, his brand nor wounds nor burns,
    And cruelty
Is sunk to hell; the fair shall all be kind;
Who loves shall be beloved, the froward mind    20
To a deformed shape shall be confined.

### IV.

Astræa hath possess'd
An earthly seat and now remains
In Finch's heart, but Wentworth's breast
    That guest contains;    25
With her she dwells, yet hath not left the skies,
Nor lost her sphere: for, new enthroned, she cries,
I know no Heaven but fair Wentworth's eyes.

## TO A. D., UNREASONABLE, DISTRUSTFUL OF HER OWN BEAUTY.

FAIR Doris, break thy glass, it hath perplex'd
With a dark comment Beauty's clearest text ;
It hath not told thy face's story true,
But brought false copies to thy jealous view.
No colour, feature, lovely air or grace,     5
That ever yet adorn'd a beauteous face,
But thou mayst read in thine ; or justly doubt
Thy glass hath been suborn'd to leave it out.
But if it offer to thy nice survey
A spot, a stain, a blemish, or decay,     10
It not belongs to thee ; the treacherous light
Or faithless stone abuse thy credulous sight.
Perhaps the magic of thy face hath wrought
Upon th' enchanted crystal, and so brought
Fantastic shadows to delude thine eyes,     15
With airy repercussive sorceries ;
Or else th' enamour'd image pines away
For love of the fair object, and so may
Wax pale and wan, and though the substance grow
Lively and fresh, that may consume with woe.     20
Give then no faith to the false specular stone,
But let thy beauties by th' effects be known.
Look, sweetest Doris, on my love-sick heart,
In that true mirror see how fair thou art !
There, by Love's never-erring pencil drawn,     25

Shalt thou behold thy face, like th' early dawn,
Shoot through the shady covert of thy hair,
Enamelling and perfuming the calm air
With pearls and roses, till thy suns display
Their lids and let out the imprison'd day ; 30
Whilst Delphic priests, enlighten'd by their theme,
In amorous numbers count thy golden beam,
And from love's altars clouds of sighs arise
In smoking incense, to adore thine eyes.
If, then, love flow from beauty, as th' effect, 35
How canst thou the resistless cause suspect?
Who would not brand that fool, that should contend
There were no fire where smoke and flames ascend?
Distrust is worse than scorn : not to believe
My harms, is greater wrong than not to grieve. 40
What cure can for my fest'ring sore be found,
Whilst thou believ'st thy beauty cannot wound?
Such humble thoughts more cruel tyrants prove
Than all the pride that e'er usurp'd in love ;
For beauty's herald here denounceth war, 45
There her false spies betray me to a snare.
If fire, disguised in balls of snow, were hurled,
It unsuspected might consume the world ;
Where our prevention ends, danger begins,
So wolves in sheeps', lions in asses' skins, 50
Might far more mischief work, because less fear'd :
Those the whole flock, these might kill all the herd.
Appear then as thou art, break through this cloud,
Confess thy beauty, though thou thence grow proud ;
Be fair, though scornful ; rather let me find 55
Thee cruel, than thus mild and more unkind.

Thy cruelty doth only me defy,
But these dull thoughts thee to thyself deny.
Whether thou mean to barter, or bestow
Thyself, 'tis fit thou thine own value know. 60
I will not cheat thee of thyself, nor pay
Less for thee than thou'rt worth ; thou shalt not say
That is but brittle glass, which I have found
By strict enquiry a firm diamond.
I'll trade with no such Indian fool, who sells 65
Gold, pearls, and precious stones, for beads and bells ;
Nor will I take a present from your hand,
Which you or prize not, or not understand.
It not endears your bounty that I do
Esteem your gift, unless you do so too : 70
You undervalue me, when you bestow
On me what you nor care for, nor yet know.
No, lovely Doris, change thy thoughts, and be
In love first with thyself, and then with me.
You are afflicted that you are not fair, 75
And I as much tormented that you are.
What I admire you scorn, what I love, hate ;
Through different faiths, both share an equal fate ;
Fast to the truth, which you renounce, I stick ;
I die a martyr, you an heretic. 80

## TO MY FRIEND G. N., FROM WREST.

I BREATHE, sweet Ghib, the temperate air of Wrest,
Where I, no more with raging storms oppress'd,
Wear the cold nights out by the banks of Tweed,
On the bleak mountains, where fierce tempests breed,
And everlasting winter dwells; where mild       5
Favonius and the vernal winds exiled,
Did never spread their wings; but the wild north
Brings sterile fern, thistles and brambles forth.
Here, steep'd in balmy dew, the pregnant earth
Sends from her teeming womb a flowery birth;   10
And, cherish'd with the warm sun's quickening heat,
Her porous bosom doth rich odours sweat;
Whose perfumes through the ambient air diffuse
Such native aromatics, as we use
No foreign gums, nor essence fetch'd from far, 15
No volatile spirits, nor compounds that are
Adulterate, but at Nature's cheap expense
With far more genuine sweets refresh the sense.
Such pure and uncompounded beauties bless
This mansion with an useful comeliness,        20
Devoid of art, for here the architect
Did not with curious skill a pile erect
Of carved marble, touch or porphyry,
But built a house for hospitality;
No sumptuous chimney-piece of shining stone    25

Invites the stranger's eye to gaze upon,
And coldly entertains his sight, but clear
And cheerful flames cherish and warm him here;
No Doric nor Corinthian pillars grace
With imagery this structure's naked face. 30
The lord and lady of this place delight
Rather to be in act, than seem in sight.
Instead of statues to adorn their wall,
They throng with living men their merry hall;
Where, at large tables fill'd with wholesome meats, 35
The servant, tenant, and kind neighbour eats.
Some of that rank, spun of a finer thread,
Are with the women, steward, and chaplain, fed
With daintier cates; others of better note,
Whom wealth, parts, office, or the herald's coat 40
Have sever'd from the common, freely sit
At the lord's table, whose spread sides admit
A large access of friends, to fill those seats
Of his capacious circle, fill'd with meats
Of choicest relish, till his oaken back 45
Under the load of piled up dishes crack.
Nor think, because our pyramids and high
Exalted turrets threaten not the sky,
That therefore Wrest of narrowness complains,
Or straiten'd walls; for she more numerous trains 50
Of noble guests daily receives, and those
Can with far more conveniency dispose,
Than prouder piles, where the vain builder spent
More cost in outward gay embellishment
Than real use; which was the sole design 55
Of our contriver, who made things not fine,

But fit for service.   Amalthea's horn
Of plenty is not in effigy worn
Without the gate, but she, within the door
Empties her free and unexhausted store ;           60
Nor, crown'd with wheaten wreaths, doth Ceres stand
In stone, with a crook'd sickle in her hand ;
Nor on a marble tun, his face besmear'd
With grapes, is curl'd unscissor'd Bacchus rear'd :
We offer not in emblems to the eyes,           65
But to the taste, those useful deities ;
We press the juicy god and quaff his blood,
And grind the yellow goddess into food.
Yet we decline not all the work of art,
But where more bounteous Nature bears a part,   70
And guides her handmaid, if she but dispense
Fit matter, she with care and diligence
Employs her skill ; for where the neighbour source
Pours forth her waters, she directs their course,
And entertains the flowing streams in deep       75
And spacious channels, where they slowly creep
In snaky windings, as the shelving ground
Leads them in circles, till they twice surround
This island mansion, which, i' th' centre placed,
Is with a double crystal heaven embraced ;        80
In which our watery constellations float,
Our fishes, swans, our water-man and boat,
Envied by those above, which wish to slake
Their star-burnt limbs in our refreshing lake ;
But they stick fast, nail'd to the barren sphere,    85
Whilst our increase in fertile waters here
Disport and wander freely where they please,

Within the circuit of our narrow seas.
With various trees we fringe the water's brink,
Whose thirsty roots the soaking moisture drink;  90
And whose extended boughs in equal ranks
Yield fruit, and shade, and beauty to the banks.
On this side young Vertumnus sits, and courts
His ruddy-cheek'd Pomona; Zephyr sports
On th' other, with loved Flora, yielding there  95
Sweets for the smell, sweets for the palate here.
But did you taste the high and mighty drink
Which from that fountain flows, you 'ld clearly think
The god of wine did his plump clusters bring
And crush the Falerne grape into our spring;  100
Or else, disguised in watery robes, did swim
To Ceres' bed, and make her big of him,
Begetting so himself on her: for know,
Our vintage here in March doth nothing owe
To theirs in autumn, but our fire boils here  105
As lusty liquor, as the sun makes there.

 Thus I enjoy myself and taste the fruit
Of this blest peace; whilst, toil'd in the pursuit
Of bucks and stags, th' emblem of war, you strive
To keep the memory of our arms alive.  110

## A NEW YEAR'S GIFT.

### TO THE KING.

Look back, old Janus, and survey
From Time's birth till this new-born day,
All the successful season bound
With laurel wreaths, and trophies crown'd;
Turn o'er the annals past, and where 5
Happy auspicious days appear,
Mark'd with the whiter stone, that cast
On the dark brow of th' ages past
A dazzling lustre, let them shine
In this succeeding circle's twine, 10
Till it be round with glories spread,
Then with it crown our Charles his head,
That we th' ensuing years may call
One great continued festival.
Fresh joys, in varied forms, apply 15
To each distinct captivity.
Season his cares by day with nights
Crown'd with all conjugal delights;
May the choice beauties that inflame
His royal breast be still the same, 20
And he still think them such, since more
Thou canst not give from Nature's store.
Then as a father let him be
With numerous issue blest, and see
The fair and god-like offspring grown 25
From budding stars to 'suns full-blown.

Circle with peaceful olive boughs
And conquering bays his regal brows;
Let his strong virtues overcome,
And bring him bloodless trophies home;  30
Strew all the pavements where he treads
With loyal hearts or rebels' heads:
But, Bifront, open thou no more
In his blest reign the temple door.


### TO THE QUEEN.

Thou great commandress, that dost move
Thy sceptre o'er the crown of Love,
And through his empire, with the awe
Of thy chaste beams, dost give the law;
From his profaner altars we  5
Turn to adore thy deity:
He only can wild lust provoke,
Thou those impurer flames canst choke;
And where he scatters looser fires,
Thou turn'st them into chaste desires;  10
His kingdom knows no rule but this,
*Whatever pleaseth, lawful is;*
Thy sacred lore shows us the path
Of modesty and constant faith,
Which makes the rude male satisfied  15

With one fair female by his side;
Doth either sex to each unite,
And form Love's pure hermaphrodite.
To this thy faith, behold the wild
Satyr already reconciled, 20
Who from the influence of thine eye
Hath suck'd the deep divinity.
O free them then, that they may teach
The Centaur and the horse-man, preach
To beasts and birds, sweetly to rest 25
Each in his proper lair and nest;
They shall convey it to the flood,
Till there thy law be understood:
  So shalt thou with thy pregnant fire
  The water, earth, and air inspire. 30


### TO THE NEW YEAR.

#### FOR THE COUNTESS OF CARLISLE.

Give Lucinda pearl nor stone;
Lend them light who else have none:
Let her beauties shine alone.

Gums nor spice bring from the East,
For the phœnix in her breast 5
Builds his funeral pile and nest.

No tire thou canst invent
Shall to grace her form be sent:
She adorns all ornament.

Give her nothing: but restore
Those sweet smiles, which heretofore
In her cheerful eyes she wore.

Drive those envious clouds away,
Veils that have o'er-cast my day,
And eclipsed her brighter ray.

Let the royal Goth mow down
This year's harvest with his own
Sword, and spare Lucinda's frown.

Janus, if when next I trace
Those sweet lines, I in her face
Read the charter of my grace,

Then from bright Apollo's tree
Such a garland wreath'd shall be,
As shall crown both her and thee.

## TO MY HONOURED FRIEND, MASTER THOMAS MAY, UPON HIS COMEDY THE HEIR.

THE HEIR being born, was in his tender age
Rock'd in the cradle of a private stage,
Where, lifted up by many a willing hand,
The child did from the first day fairly stand;
Since, having gather'd strength, he dares prefer   5
His steps into the public theatre,
The world: where he despairs not but to find
A doom from men more able, not less kind.

  I but his usher am, yet if my word
May pass, I dare be bound he will afford         10
Things must deserve a welcome, if well known,
Such as best writers would have wish'd their own.

  You shall observe his words in order meet,
And softly stealing on with equal feet,
Slide into equal numbers with such grace         15
As each word had been moulded for that place.

  You shall perceive an amorous passion spun
Into so smooth a web, as had the sun,
When he pursued the swiftly flying maid,
Courted her in such language, she had stay'd;    20
A love so well express'd must be the same
The author felt himself from his fair flame.

  The whole plot doth alike itself disclose
Through the five acts, as doth the lock that goes
With letters, for, till every one be known,      25
The lock's as fast as if you had found none.

And where his sportive muse doth draw a thread
Of mirth, chaste matrons may not blush to read.
  Thus have I thought it fitter to reveal
My want of art, dear friend, than to conceal   30
My love. It did appear I did not mean
So to commend thy well-wrought comic scene,
As men might judge my aim rather to be
To gain praise to myself, than give it thee :
Though I can give thee none but what thou hast 35
Deserv'd, and what must my faint breath out-last.
  Yet was this garment (though I skill-less be
To take thy measure), only made for thee,
And if it prove too scant, 'tis 'cause the stuff
Nature allow'd me was not large enough.   40

### TO MY WORTHY FRIEND MASTER GEORGE SANDYS, ON HIS TRANSLATION OF THE PSALMS.

I PRESS not to the choir, nor dare I greet
The holy place with my unhallow'd feet ;
My unwash'd Muse pollutes not things divine
Nor mingles her profaner notes with thine ;
Here humbly at the porch she stays,   5
And with glad ears sucks in thy sacred lays.
So devout penitents of old were wont,
Some without door and some beneath the font,
To stand and hear the Church's liturgies,
Yet not assist the solemn exercise.   10
Sufficeth her, that she a lay-place gain,

To trim thy vestments, or but bear thy train;
Though nor in tune nor wing she reach thy lark,
Her lyric feet may dance before the Ark.
Who knows, but that her wand'ring eyes, that run 15
Now hunting glow-worms, may adore the sun?
A pure flame may, shot by Almighty power
Into her breast, the earthy flame devour?
My eyes in penitential dew may steep
That brine, which they for sensual love did weep. 20
So, though 'gainst Nature's course, fire may be quench'd
With fire, and water be with water drench'd,
Perhaps my restless soul, tired with pursuit
Of mortal beauty, seeking without fruit
Contentment there, which hath not, when enjoy'd 25
Quench'd all her thirst, nor satisfied, though cloy'd,
Weary of her vain search below, above
In the first fair may find th' immortal love.
Prompted by thy example then, no more
In moulds of clay will I my God adore; 30
But tear those idols from my heart, and write
What his blest Spirit, not fond love, shall indite.
Then I no more shall court the verdant bay,
But the dry leafless trunk on Golgotha,
And rather strive to gain from thence one thorn, 35
Than all the flourishing wreaths by Laureates worn.

l. 32.   Old edition, *Sprit.*

TO MY MUCH HONOURED FRIEND, HENRY, LORD CAREY OF LEPPINGTON, UPON HIS TRANSLATION OF MALVEZZI.

My Lord, in every trivial work, 'tis known,
Translators must be masters of their own
And of their author's language, but your task
A greater latitude of skill did ask;
For your Malvezzi first required a man  5
To teach him speak vulgar Italian;
His matter's so sublime, so now his phrase
So far above the style of Bembo's days,
Old Varchi's rules, or what the Crusca yet
For current Tuscan mintage will admit,  10
As I believe, your Marquess, by a good
Part of his natives, hardly understood.
You must expect no happier fate; 'tis true,
He is of noble birth, of nobler you:
So nor your thoughts nor words fit common ears;  15
He writes, and you translate, both to your peers.

## TO MY WORTHY FRIEND, MASTER DAVENANT UPON HIS EXCELLENT PLAY, THE JUST ITALIAN.

I'LL not mis-spend in praise the narrow room
I borrow in this lease; the garlands bloom
From thine own seeds, that crown each glorious page
Of thy triumphant work; the sullen age
Requires a satire. What star guides the soul    5
Of these our froward times, that dare control,
Yet dare not learn to judge? When didst thou fly
From hence, clear candid Ingenuity?
I have beheld when, perch'd on the smooth brow
Of a fair modest troop, thou didst allow    10
Applause to slighter works; but then the weak
Spectator gave the knowing leave to speak.
Now noise prevails, and he is tax'd for drouth
Of wit, that with the cry spends not his mouth.
Yet ask him reason why he did not like,    15
Him, why he did; their ignorance will strike
Thy soul with scorn and pity. Mark the places
Provoke their smiles, frowns, or distorted faces;
When they admire, nod, shake the head; they'll be
A scene of mirth, a double comedy.    20
But thy strong fancies (raptures of the brain,
Dress'd in poetic flames,) they entertain
As a bold impious reach; for they'll still slight

All that exceeds Red Bull and Cock-pit flight.
 These are the men in crowded heap that throng 25
To that adulterate stage, where not a tongue
Of th' untuned kennel can a line repeat
Of serious sense, but like lips meet like meat:
Whilst the true brood of actors, that alone
Keep natural unstrain'd action in her throne,   30
Behold their benches bare, though they rehearse
The terser Beaumont's or great Jonson's verse.
Repine not thou, then, since this churlish fate
Rules not the stage alone; perhaps the State
Hath felt this rancour, where men great and good 35
Have by the rabble been misunderstood.
So was thy play, whose clear yet lofty strain
Wise men, that govern Fate, shall entertain.

## TO THE READER OF
## MASTER WILLIAM DAVENANT'S PLAY.

It hath been said of old that plays are feasts,
Poets the cooks, and the spectators guests,
The actors waiters: from this simile
Some have derived an unsafe liberty,
To use their judgments as their tastes, which choose 5
Without control this dish, and that refuse.
But wit allows not this large privilege:
Either you must confess or feel its edge.
Nor shall you make a current inference,

If you transfer your reason to your sense: 10
Things are distinct, and must the same appear
To every piercing eye or well-tuned ear.
Though sweets with yours, sharps best with my
    taste meet,
Both must agree this meat's or sharp or sweet:
But if I scent a stench or a perfume, 15
Whilst you smell nought at all, I may presume
You have that sense imperfect: so you may
Affect a sad, merry, or humorous play,
If, though the kind distaste or please, the good
And bad be by your judgment understood. 20
But if, as in this play, where with delight
I feast my Epicurean appetite
With relishes so curious, as dispense
The utmost pleasure to the ravish'd sense,
You should profess that you can nothing meet 25
That hits your taste either with sharp or sweet,
But cry out, 'Tis insipid! your bold tongue
May do its master, not the author, wrong;
For men of better palate will by it
Take the just elevation of your wit. 30

## TO MY FRIEND,
### WILL. DAVENANT.

When I behold, by warrant from thy pen,
A prince rigging our fleets, arming our men,
Conducting to remotest shores our force,
(Without a Dido to retard his course)
And thence repelling in successful fight      5
Th' usurping foe, whose strength was all his right,
By two brave heroes (whom we justly may
By Homer's Ajax or Achilles lay):
I doubt the author of the Tale of Troy,
With him that makes his fugitive enjoy      10
The Carthage Queen, and think thy poem may
Impose upon posterity, as they
Have done on us.  What though romances lie
Thus blended with more faithful history?
We of th' adult'rate mixture not complain,      15
But thence more characters of virtue gain;
More pregnant patterns of transcendent worth,
Than barren and insipid Truth brings forth:
So oft the bastard nobler fortune meets
Than the dull issue of the lawful sheets.      20

ll. 1—14 not in the editions: see Notes.

## THE COMPARISON.

Dearest, thy tresses are not threads of gold,
Thy eyes of diamonds, nor do I hold
Thy lips for rubies, thy fair cheeks to be
Fresh roses, or thy teeth of ivory;
The skin that doth thy dainty body sheathe       5
Not alablaster is, nor dost thou breathe
Arabian odours; those the earth brings forth,
Compared with which would but impair thy worth.
Such may be others' mistresses, but mine
Holds nothing earthly, but is all divine.       10
Thy tresses are those rays that do arise
Not from one sun, but two; such are thy eyes:
Thy lips congealed nectar are, and such
As (but a deity) there's none dare touch.
The perfect crimson that thy cheek doth clothe  15
(But only that it far excels them both,)
Aurora's blush resembles, or that red
That frisketh in when her mantle's spread.
Thy teeth in white do Leda's swan exceed;
Thy skin's a heavenly and immortal weed;        20
And when thou breath'st, the winds are ready straight
To filch it from thee, and do therefore wait
Close at thy lips, and snatching it from thence,
Bear it to heaven, where 'tis Jove's frankincense.
Fair Goddess, since thy feature makes thee one, 25
Yet be not such for these respects alone;
But as you are divine in outward view,
So be within as fair, as good, as true.

l. 21. Original edition, *And thou when breath'st*.

## THE COMPLEMENT.

O MY dearest, I shall grieve thee,
When I swear (yet, sweet, believe me,)
By thine eyes, the tempting book
On which even crabb'd old men look,
I swear to thee, though none abhor them,   5
Yet I do not love thee for them.

I do not love thee for that fair
Rich fan of thy most curious hair;
Though the wires thereof be drawn
Finer than the threads of lawn,   10
And are softer than the leaves
On which the subtle spinner weaves.

I do not love thee for those flowers
Growing on thy cheeks (Love's bowers);
Though such cunning them hath spread,   15
None can paint their white and red;
Love's golden arrows thence are shot,
Yet for them I love thee not.

I do not love thee for those soft
Red coral lips I've kiss'd so oft;   20
Nor teeth of pearl, the double guard
To speech, whence music still is heard;

l. 16. Original edition, *paint them*.

Though from those lips a kiss being taken
Might tyrants melt, and death awaken.

I do not love thee, O my fairest!  25
For that richest, for that rarest
Silver pillar which stands under
Thy sound head, that globe of wonder;
Though that neck be whiter far
Than towers of polish'd ivory are.  30

I do not love thee for those mountains
Hill'd with snow, whence milky fountains
(Sugar'd sweets, as syrup'd berries),
Must one day run through pipes of cherries:
O how much those breasts do move me!  35
Yet for them I do not love thee.

I do not love thee for that belly,
Sleek as satin, soft as jelly;
Though within that crystal round
Heaps of treasure might be found,  40
So rich, that for the best of them
A king might leave his diadem.

I do not love thee for those thighs,
Whose alabaster rocks do rise
So high and even, that they stand  45
Like sea-marks to some happy land:
Happy are those eyes have seen them,
More happy they that sail between them.

44. The editions have *use* for *rise*.

I love thee not for thy moist palm,
Though the dew thereof be balm; 50
Nor for thy pretty leg and foot,
Although it be the precious root,
On which this goodly cedar grows:
Sweet, I love thee not for those.

Nor for thy wit, though pure and quick, 55
Whose substance no arithmetic
Can number down; nor for those charms
Mask'd in thy embracing arms,
Though in them one night to lie,
Dearest, I would gladly die. 60

I love not for those eyes, nor hair,
Nor cheeks, nor lips, nor teeth so rare,
Nor for thy speech, thy neck, nor breast,
Nor for thy belly, nor the rest,
Nor for thy hand nor foot so small: 65
But, wouldst thou know, dear sweet, for all.

## ON SIGHT OF A GENTLEWOMAN'S FACE IN THE WATER.

STAND still, you floods! do not deface
    That image which you bear;
So votaries from every place
    To you shall altars rear.

No winds but lovers' sighs blow here,     5
    To trouble these glad streams,
On which no star from any sphere
    Did ever dart such beams.

To crystal then in haste congeal,
    Lest you should lose your bliss;     10
And to my cruel fair reveal
    How cold, how hard she is!

But if the envious nymphs shall fear
    Their beauties will be scorn'd,
And hire the ruder winds to tear     15
    That face which you adorn'd,

Then rage and foam amain, that we
    Their malice may despise;
When from your froth we soon shall see
    A second Venus rise.     20

## A SONG.

Ask me no more where Jove bestows,
When June is past, the fading rose;
For in your beauty's orient deep
These flowers, as in their causes, sleep.

Ask me no more whither do stray       5
The golden atoms of the day;
For in pure love heaven did prepare
Those powders to enrich your hair.

Ask me no more whither doth haste
The nightingale, when May is past;    10
For in your sweet dividing throat
She winters, and keeps warm her note.

Ask me no more where those stars 'light,
That downwards fall in dead of night;
For in your eyes they sit, and there  15
Fixed become, as in their sphere.

Ask me no more if east or west
The phœnix builds her spicy nest;
For unto you at last she flies,
And in your fragrant bosom dies.      20

## THE SECOND RAPTURE.

No, worldling, no, 'tis not thy gold,
Which thou dost use but to behold,
Nor fortune, honour, nor long life,
Children, or friends, nor a good wife,
That makes thee happy: these things be    5
But shadows of felicity.
Give me a wench about thirteen,
Already voted to the queen
Of lust and lovers; whose soft hair
Fann'd with the breath of gentle air,    10
O'er-spreads her shoulders like a tent,
And is her veil and ornament;
Whose tender touch will make the blood
Wild in the aged and the good;
Whose kisses, fasten'd to the mouth    15
Of three-score years and longer slouth,
Renew the age; and whose bright eye
Obscures those lesser lights of sky;
Whose snowy breasts (if we may call
That snow, that never melts at all,)    20
Makes Jove invent a new disguise,
In spite of Juno's jealousies;
Whose every part doth re-invite
The old decayed appetite;
And in whose sweet embraces I    25
May melt my self to lust, and die.
  This is true bliss, and I confess
  There is no other happiness.

I

### THE TINDER.

Of what mould did Nature frame me,
Or was it her intent to shame me,
That no woman can come near me,
Fair, but her I court to hear me?
Sure that mistress, to whose beauty 5
First I paid a lover's duty,
Burn'd in rage my heart to tinder,
That nor prayers nor tears can hinder,
But wherever I do turn me,
Every spark let fall doth burn me; 10
Women, since you thus inflame me,
Flint and steel I'll ever name ye.

## A SONG.

In her fair cheeks two pits do lie,
To bury those slain by her eye;
So, spite of death, this comforts me,
That fairly buried I shall be,
My grave with rose and lily spread;  5
O 'tis a life to be so dead!
    Come then, and kill me with thy eye,
    For, if thou let me live, I die.

When I behold those lips again,
Reviving what those eyes have slain,  10
With kisses sweet, whose balsam pure
Love's wounds, as soon as made, can cure,
Methinks 'tis sickness to be sound,
And there's no health to such a wound.
    Come then, and kill me with thy eye,  15
    For, if thou let me live, I die.

When in her chaste breast I behold
Those downy mounts of snow, ne'er cold;
And those blest hearts her beauty kills,
Revived by climbing those fair hills,  20

Methinks there's life in such a death,
And so t' expire inspires new breath.
    Come then, and kill me with thy eye:
    For, if thou let me live, I die.

Nymph, since no death is deadly, where   25
Such choice of antidotes are near,
And your keen eyes but kill in vain
Those that are sound, as soon as slain;
That I, no longer dead, survive,
Your way's to bury me alive           30
In Cupid's cave, where happy I
May dying live, and living die.
    Come then, and kill me with thy eye:
    For, if thou let me live, I die.

## THE CARVER.

### TO HIS MISTRESS.

A CARVER, having loved too long in vain,
   Hew'd out the portraiture of Venus' son
In marble rock, upon the which did rain
   Small drizzling drops, that from a fount did run;
Imagining the drops would either wear      5
   His fury out, or quench his living flame:
But when he saw it bootless did appear,
   He swore the water did augment the same.
So I, that seek in verse to carve thee out,
   Hoping thy beauty will my flame allay,      10
Viewing my lines impolish'd all throughout,
   Find my will rather to my love obey:
That with the carver I my work do blame,
   Finding it still th' augmenter of my flame.

## TO THE PAINTER.

FOND man, that hop'st to catch that face
With those false colours, whose short grace
Serves but to show the lookers-on
The faults of thy presumption;
Or, at the least, to let us see 5
That is divine, but yet not she:
Say, you could imitate the rays
Of those eyes that outshine the days,
Or counterfeit in red and white
That most uncounterfeited light 10
Of her complexion; yet canst thou,
Great master though thou be, tell how
To paint a virtue? Then desist,
This fair your artifice hath miss'd.
You should have mark'd how she begins 15
To grow in virtue, not in sins;
Instead of that same rosy dye,
You should have drawn out modesty,
Whose beauty sits enthroned there,
And learn to look and blush at her. 20
Or can you colour just the same,
When virtue blushes, or when shame?
When sickness, and when innocence,
Shows pale or white unto the sense?
Can such coarse varnish e'er be said 25
To imitate her white and red?
This may do well elsewhere, in Spain,

Among those faces dyed in grain;
So you may thrive, and what you do
Prove the best picture of the two. 30
Besides, if all I hear be true,
'Tis taken ill by some that you
Should be so insolently vain,
As to contrive all that rich gain
Into one tablet, which alone 35
May teach us superstition,
Instructing our amazed eyes
To admire and worship imag'ries,
Such as quickly might outshine
Some new saint, were 't allow'd a shrine, 40
And turn each wand'ring looker-on
Into a new Pygmalion.
Yet your art cannot equalize
This picture in her lover's eyes;
His eyes the pencils are which limn 45
Her truly, as hers copy him;
His heart the tablet, which alone
Is for that portrait the tru'st stone.
If you would a truer see,
Mark it in their posterity: 50
And you shall read it truly there,
When the glad world shall see their heir.

## LOVE'S COURTSHIP.

Kiss, lovely Celia, and be kind;
Let my desires freedom find,
    Sit thee down,
And we will make the gods confess
Mortals enjoy some happiness.     5

Mars would disdain his mistress' charms
If he beheld thee in my arms,
    And descend,
Thee his mortal queen to make,
Or live as mortal for thy sake.     10

Venus must lose her title now,
And leave to brag of Cupid's bow;
    Silly Queen!
She hath but one, but I can spy
Ten thousand Cupids in thy eye.     15

Nor may the sun behold our bliss,
For sure thy eyes do dazzle his;
    If thou fear
That he'll betray thee with his light,
Let me eclipse thee from his sight!     20

And while I shade thee from his eye
Oh! let me hear thee gently cry,
    Celia yields!
Maids often lose their maidenhead,
Ere they set foot in nuptial bed.     25

## ON A DAMASK ROSE, STICKING UPON A LADY'S BREAST.

LET pride grow big, my rose, and let the clear
And damask colour of thy leaves appear;
Let scent and looks be sweet, and bless that hand
That did transplant thee to that sacred land.
O happy thou! that in that garden rest'st,  5
That, paradise between that lady's breasts.
There's an eternal spring; there shalt thou lie
Betwixt two lily mounts, and never die.
There shalt thou spring amongst the fertile valleys,
By buds, like thee, that grow in 'midst of alleys.  10
There none dare pluck thee, for that place is such,
That, but a good divine, there's none dare touch.
If any but approach, straight doth arise
A blushing lightning flash and blasts his eyes.
There, 'stead of rain, shall living fountains flow,  15
For wind, her fragrant breath for ever blow:
Nor now, as erst, one sun shall on thee shine,
But those two glorious suns, her eyes divine.
O then, what monarch would not think 't a grace
To leave his regal throne to have thy place?  20
Myself, to gain thy blessed seat, do vow,
Would be transform'd into a rose, as thou.

### THE PROTESTATION: A SONNET.

No more shall meads be deck'd with flowers,
Nor sweetness dwell in rosy bowers,
Nor greenest buds on branches spring,
Nor warbling birds delight to sing,
Nor April violets paint the grove, 5
If I forsake my Celia's love.

The fish shall in the ocean burn,
And fountains sweet shall bitter turn;
The humble oak no flood shall know,
When floods shall highest hills o'er-flow; 10
Black Lethe shall oblivion leave,
If e'er my Celia I deceive.

Love shall his bow and shaft lay by,
And Venus' doves want wings to fly;
The sun refuse to show his light, 15
And day shall then be turn'd to night;
And in that night no star appear,
If once I leave my Celia dear.

Love shall no more inhabit earth,
Nor lovers more shall love for worth, 20
Nor joy above in heaven dwell,
Nor pain torment poor souls in hell;
Grim death no more shall horrid prove,
If e'er I leave bright Celia's love.

## THE TOOTH-ACHE CURED BY A KISS.

FATE'S now grown merciful to men,
    Turning disease to bliss;
For had not kind rheum vext me then,
    I might not Celia kiss.
Physicians, you are now my scorn, 5
    For I have found a way
To cure diseases, when forlorn
    By your dull art, which may
Patch up a body for a time,
    But can restore to health 10
No more than chemists can sublime
    True gold, the Indies' wealth.
That angel sure, that used to move
    The pool men so admired,
Hath to her lip, the seat of love, 15
    As to his heaven, retired.

## TO HIS JEALOUS MISTRESS.

ADMIT, thou darling of mine eyes,
   I have some idol lately framed,
That under such a false disguise
   Our true loves might the less be famed:
Canst thou, that knowest my heart, suppose     5
I'll fall from thee, and worship those?

Remember, dear, how loth and slow
   I was to cast a look or smile,
Or one love-line to misbestow,
   Till thou hadst changed both face and style:   10
And art thou grown afraid to see
That mask put on thou mad'st for me?

I dare not call those childish fears,
   Coming from love, much less from thee;
But wash away, with frequent tears,     15
   This counterfeit idolatry:
And henceforth kneel at ne'er a shrine,
To blind the world, but only thine.

### THE DART.

OFT when I look I may descry
    A little face peep through that eye;
Sure, that's the boy, which wisely chose
His throne among such beams as those,
Which, if his quiver chance to fall,
May serve for darts to kill withal.

## THE MISTAKE.

WHEN on fair Celia I did spy
    A wounded heart of stone,
The wound had almost made me cry,
    Sure this heart was my own!

But when I saw it was enthroned
    In her celestial breast,
O then I it no longer own'd,
    For mine was ne'er so blest.

Yet, if in highest heavens do shine,
    Each constant martyr's heart,
Then she may well give rest to mine,
    That for her sake doth smart;

Where, seated in so high a bliss,
    Though wounded, it shall live;
Death enters not in Paradise,
    The place free life doth give.

Or if the place less sacred were,
    Did but her saving eye
Bathe my sick heart in one kind tear,
    Then should I never die.

Slight balms may heal a slighter sore,
    No medicine less divine
Can ever hope for to restore
    A wounded heart like mine.

## ON MISTRESS N.

### TO THE GREEN SICKNESS.

Stay, coward blood, and do not yield
To thy pale sister beauty's field,
Who, there displaying round her white
Ensigns, hath usurp'd thy night,
Invading thy peculiar throne, 5
The lip, where thou shouldst rule alone;
And on the cheek, where Nature's care
Allotted each an equal share,
Her spreading lily only grows,
Whose milky deluge drowns thy rose. 10
   Quit not the field, faint blood, nor rush
In the short sally of a blush
Upon thy sister foe, but strive
To keep an endless war alive:
Though peace do petty states maintain, 15
Here war alone makes beauty reign.

## UPON A MOLE IN CELIA'S BOSOM.

That lovely spot, which thou dost see
In Celia's bosom, was a bee
Who built her amorous spicy nest
In th' Hyblas of her either breast.
But from close ivory hives she flew       5
To suck the aromatic dew,
Which from the neighbour vale distils,
Which parts those two twin-sister hills.
There feasting on ambrosial meat,
A rolling file of balmy sweat             10
(As in soft murmurs before death
Swan-like she sung), choked up her breath:
So she in water did expire,
More precious than the Phœnix fire.

   Yet still her shadow there remains,   15
Confined to those Elysian plains,
With this strict law, that who shall lay
His bold lips on that milky way,
The sweet and smart from thence shall bring
Of the bee's honey and her sting.         20

### AN HYMENEAL SONG, ON THE NUPTIALS OF THE LADY ANN WENTWORTH AND THE LORD LOVELACE.

BREAK not the slumbers of the bride,
But let the sun in triumph ride,
   Scattering his beamy light;
When she awakes, he shall resign
His rays, and she alone shall shine      5
   In glory all the night.

For she, till day return, must keep
An amorous vigil, and not steep
Her fair eyes in the dew of sleep.

Yet gently whisper, as she lies,      10
And say her lord waits her uprise,
   The priests at the altar stay:
With flow'ry wreaths the virgin crew
Attend, while some with roses strew,
   And myrtles trim the way.      15

Now to the temple and the priest
See her convey'd, thence to the feast;
Then back to bed, though not to rest.

l. 17. The 1642 edition in which this song first appeared reads *fast* for *feast*. The misprint was corrected in the 1651 edition.

For now, to crown his faith and truth,
We must admit the noble youth 20
    To revel in Love's sphere;
To rule, as chief intelligence,
That orb, and happy time dispense
    To wretched lovers here;

For there exalted far above 25
All hope, fear, change, are they to move
The wheel that spins the fates of Love.

They know no night, nor glaring noon,
Measure no hours of sun or moon,
    Nor mark Time's restless glass; 30
Their kisses measure as they flow
Minutes, and their embraces show
    The hours as they pass.

Their motions the year's circle make,
And we from their conjunctions take 35
Rules to make Love an almanac.

l. 26. The old copies read *or they* to move.

### A MARRIED WOMAN.

WHEN I shall marry, if I do not find
A wife thus moulded, I'll create this mind:
Nor from her noble birth, nor ample dower,
Beauty, or wit, shall she derive a power
To prejudice my right; but if she be      5
A subject born, she shall be so to me.
As to the soul the flesh, as appetite
To reason is, which shall our wills unite,
In habits so confirm'd, as no rough sway
Shall once appear, if she but learns t' obey.   10
For in habitual virtues sense is wrought
To that calm temper, as the body's thought
To have nor blood nor gall, if wild and rude
Passions of lust and anger are subdued;
When 'tis the fair obedience to the soul   15
Doth in the birth those swelling acts control.
If I in murder steep my furious rage,
Or with adult'ry my hot lust assuage,
Will it suffice to say my sense, the beast,
Provoked me to 't? Could I my soul divest,   20
My plea were good. Lions and bulls commit
Both freely, but man must in judgment sit,
And tame this beast; for Adam was not free
When in excuse he said, Eve gave it me;
Had he not eaten, she perhaps had been    25
Unpunish'd: his consent made her's a sin.

### A DIVINE LOVE.

WHY should dull Art, which is wise Nature's ape,
   If she produce a shape,
So far beyond all patterns that of old
   Fell from her mould,
As thine, admired Lucinda, not bring forth    5
An equal wonder to express that worth
   In some new way, that hath
Like her great work no print of vulgar path?

Is it because the rapes of Poetry,
   Rifling the spacious sky    10
Of all his fires, light, beauty, influence,
   Did those dispense
On airy creations, that surpass'd
The real works of Nature; she at last,
   To prove their raptures vain,    15
Show'd such a light as poets could not feign?

Or is it 'cause the factious wits did vie
   With vain idolatry,
Whose goddess was supreme, and so had hurl'd
   Schism through the world,    20
Whose priest sung sweetest lays, thou didst appear,
A glorious mystery, so dark, so clear,
   As Nature did intend
All should confess, but none might comprehend?

Perhaps all other beauties share a light    25
   Proportion'd to the sight
Of weak mortality; scattering such loose fires
   As stir desires,

And from the brain distil salt amorous rheums;
Whilst thy immortal flame such dross consumes,   30
        And from the earthy mould
With purging fires severs the purer gold?
If so, then why in Fame's immortal scroll
        Do we their names enroll,
Whose easy hearts and wanton eyes did sweat   35
        With sensual heat?
If Petrarch's unarm'd bosom catch a wound
From a light glance, must Laura be renown'd?
        Or both a glory gain,
He from ill-govern'd love, she from disdain?   40

Shall he more famed in his great art become,
        For wilful martyrdom?
Shall she more title gain, too chaste and fair,
        Through his despair?
Is Troy more noble 'cause to ashes turn'd,   45
Than virgin cities that yet never burn'd?
        Is fire, when it consumes
Temples, more fire, than when it melts perfumes?

'Cause Venus from the ocean took her form,
        Must love needs be a storm?   50
'Cause she her wanton shrines in islands rears,
        Through seas of tears,
O'er rocks and gulfs, with our own sighs for gale,
Must we to Cyprus or to Paphos sail?
        Can there no way be given,   55
But a true hell, that leads to her false heaven?

  l. 43. Quy. "Shall she more title gain to chaste and fair?"
  l. 52. The 1642 edition has *leas* for *seas*.

## LOVE'S FORCE.

IN the first ruder age, when Love was wild,
Nor yet by laws reclaim'd, not reconciled
To order, nor by Reason mann'd, but flew
Full-summ'd by Nature, on the instant view
Upon the wings of Appetite, at all                 5
The eye could fair, or sense delightful call;
Election was not yet: but as their cheap
Food from the oak, or the next acorn-heap,
As water from the nearest spring or brook,
So men their undistinguish'd females took         10
By chance, not choice: but soon the heavenly spark,
That in man's bosom lurk'd, broke through this dark
Confusion: then the noblest breast first felt
Itself for its own proper object melt.

## A FANCY.

Mark how this polish'd Eastern sheet
Doth with our Northern tincture meet,
For though the paper seem to sink,
Yet it receives and bears the ink;
And on her smooth soft brow these spots   5
Seem rather ornaments than blots,
Like those you ladies use to place
Mysteriously about your face,
Not only to set off and break
Shadows and eye-beams, but to speak   10
To the skill'd lover, and relate
Unheard his sad or happy fate.
Nor do their characters delight
As careless works of black and white;
But 'cause you underneath may find   15
A sense that can inform the mind,
Divine or moral rules impart,
Or raptures of poetic art:
So what at first was only fit
To fold up silks, may wrap up wit.   20

## TO HIS MISTRESS.

Grieve not, my Celia, but with haste
   Obey the fury of thy fate;
'Tis some perfection to waste
   Discreetly out our wretched state:
To be obedient in this sense                     5
Will prove thy virtue, though offence.

Who knows but destiny may relent?
   For many miracles have been:
Thou proving thus obedient
   To all the griefs she plunged thee in:     10
And then, the certainty she meant
Reverted is, by accident.

But yet, I must confess, 'tis much,
   When we remember what hath been:
Thus parting, never more to touch,            15
   To let eternal absence in:
Though never was our pleasure yet
So pure, but chance distracted it.

What, shall we then submit to Fate,
   And die to one another's love?              20
No, Celia, no, my soul doth hate
   Those lovers that inconstant prove.
Fate may be cruel, but if you decline,
The crime is yours, and all the glory mine.

   Fate and the planets sometimes bodies
      part,                                             25
   But canker'd nature only alters th' heart.

### IN PRAISE OF HIS MISTRESS.

You that will a wonder know,
    Go with me;
Two suns in a heaven of snow
    Both burning be:
All they fire, that but eye them,    5
But the snow's unmelted by them.

Leaves of crimson tulips met,
    Guide the way
Where two pearly rows be set,
    As white as day:    10
When they part themselves asunder,
She breathes oracles of wonder.

Hills of milk, with azure mix'd,
    Swell beneath,
Waving sweetly, yet still fix'd,    15
    While she doth breathe:
From those hills descends a valley,
Where all fall, that dare to dally.

As fair pillars, under stand
    Statues two;    20

Whiter than the silver swan
    That swims in Po:
If at any time they move her,
Every step begets a lover.

All this but the casket is, 25
    Which contains
Such a jewel, as the miss
    Breeds endless pains;
That's her mind, and they that know it,
May admire, but cannot show it. 30

## TO CELIA, UPON LOVE'S UBIQUITY.

As one that strives, being sick, and sick to death,
By changing places to preserve a breath,
A tedious restless breath, removes, and tries
A thousand rooms, a thousand policies,
To cozen pain, when he thinks to find ease:  5
At last he finds all change, but his disease.
So, like a ball with fire and powder fill'd,
I restless am, yet live, each minute kill'd,
And, with that moving torture must retain,
With change of all things else, a constant pain.  10
Say I stay with you, presence is to me
Nought but a light to show my misery;
And partings are as racks to plague love on,
The further stretch'd, the more affliction.
Go I to Holland, France, or farthest Ind,  15
I change but only countries, not my mind:
And though I pass through air and water free,
Despair and hopeless fate still follow me.
Whilst in the bosom of the waves I reel,
My heart I'll liken to the tottering keel,  20
The sea to my own troubled fate, the wind
To your disdain, sent from a soul unkind.
But when I lift my sad looks to the skies,
Then shall I think I see my Celia's eyes;

l. 13. The 1651 edition has *parting* for *partings*.

And when a cloud or storm appears between,   25
I shall remember what her frowns have been.
Thus, whatsoever course my Fates allow,
All things but make me mind my business, you.
The good things that I meet, I think streams be,
From you, the fountain; but when bad I see,   30
How vile and cursed is that thing, think I,
That to such goodness is so contrary.
My whole life is 'bout you, the centre star,
But a perpetual motion circular.
I am the dial's hand, still walking round,   35
You are the compass: and I never sound
Beyond your circle, neither can I show
Aught, but what first expressed is in you:
That, wheresoe'er my tears do cause me move,
My fate still keeps me bounded with your love;   40
Which, ere it die or be extinct in me,
Time shall stand still, and moist waves flaming be.
Yet, being gone, think not on me: I am
A thing too wretched for thy thoughts to name:
But when I die, and wish all comforts given,   45
I'll think on you, and by you think on heaven.

## TO MISTRESS KATHERINE NEVILLE, ON HER GREEN SICKNESS.

WHITE Innocence, that now liest spread,
Forsaken on thy widow'd bed,
Cold and alone, if fear, love, hate,
Or shame recall thy crimson mate,      5
From his dark mazes to reside
With thee his chaste and maiden bride:
And lest he backward thence should flow,
Congeal him with thy virgin snow.
But if his own heat, with thy pair
Of neighbouring suns and flaming hair,      10
Thaw him into a new divorce;
Lest to the heart he take his course,
Oh, lodge me there, where I'll defeat
All future hopes of his retreat,
And force the fugitive to seek      15
A constant station in thy cheek.
So each shall keep his proper place,
I in your heart, he in your face.

## MR. CAREW TO HIS FRIEND.

LIKE to the hand, that hath been used to play
One lesson long, still runs the self-same way,
And waits not what the heavens bid it strike,
But doth presume by Custom 'this will like:'
So run my thoughts, which are so perfect grown,   5
So well acquainted with my passion,
That now they dare prevent me with their haste,
And ere I think to sigh, my sigh is past :
It's past and flown to you, for you alone
Are all the object that I think upon :   10
And did you not supply my soul with thought,
For want of action it to none were brought.
What though, our absent arms may not enfold
Real embraces, yet we firmly hold
Each other in possession ; thus we see   15
The lord enjoys his land, where'er he be.
If kings possess'd no more than where they sate,
What were they greater than a mean estate?
This makes me firmly yours, you firmly mine,
That something more than bodies us combine.   20

## TO HIS MISTRESS RETIRING IN AFFECTION.

FLY not from him whose silent misery
Breathes many an unwitness'd sigh to thee,
Who having felt thy scorn, yet constant is,
And whom thou hast thyself called only his.
   When first mine eyes threw flames, whose
      spirit moved thee,     5
   Had'st thou not look'd again I had not loved
      thee.

Nature did ne'er two different things unite
With peace, which are by Nature opposite.
If thou force Nature, and be backward gone,   9
O, blame not me, that strive to draw thee on:
   But if my constant love shall fail to move thee,
   Then know my reason hates thee, though I
      love thee.

# POEMS

By THOMAS CAREY.

## ON HIS MISTRESS GOING TO SEA.

FAREWELL, fair Saint! may not the sea and wind
Swell like the hearts and eyes you leave behind;
But calm and gentle, as the looks you bear,
Smile in your face, and whisper in your ear.

   Let no bold billow offer to arise,         5
That it may nearer gaze upon your eyes:
Lest wind and wave, enamour'd of your form,
Should throng and crowd themselves into a storm.

   But if it be your fate, vast seas! to love,
Of my becalmed breast learn how to move;       10
Move then, but in a gentle lover's pace:
No wrinkle, nor no furrow, in your face.

   And you, fierce winds, see that you tell your tale
In such a breath as may but fill her sail;
So, whilst you court her, each your several way, 15
You may her safely to her port convey,
     And loose her by the noblest way of wooing:
     Whilst both contribute to your own undoing.

## METHODUS AMANDI.

*A Dialogue.*

### I.

Tell me, Eutresia, since my fate,
   And thy more powerful form, decrees
My heart an immolation at thy shrine,
Where it is ever to incline,
How I must love, and at what rate;     5
   And by what steps, and what degrees,
I shall my hopes enlarge, or my desires confine.

[*She replies.*]

   First, when thy flames begin,
   See they burn all within;
And so, as lookers-on may not descry     10
Smoke in a sigh, or sparkle in an eye.
   I'd have thy love a good while there,
   Ere thine own heart should be aware:
And I myself would choose to know it,
First by thy care and cunning not to show it.  15

[*He pleads.*]

When my flame, thine own way, is thus betray'd,
   Must it be still afraid?
May it not be sharp-sighted too, as well,
And know thou know'st, that which it dares not tell?
   And, by that knowledge, find it may     20
   Tell itself o'er, a louder way?

## II.

### [*Her truce.*]

Let me alone, a while!
For so thou mayest beguile
My heart to a consent,
Long ere it meant.                              25
For while I dare not disapprove,
Lest that betray a knowledge of thy love,
I shall be so accustom'd to allow,
That I shall not know how
To be displeased, when thou shalt it avow.      30

## III.

### [*He argues.*]

When by Love's powerful secret sympathy
Our souls are got thus nigh,
And that, by one another seen,
There needs no breath to go between;
Though in the main agreement of our breasts,    35
Our hearts subscribe as interests,
Will it not need
The tongues' sign too, as witness to the deed?

### [*She yields.*]

Speak, then! but when you whisper out the tale
Of what you ail,                                40
Let it be so disorder'd that I may
Guess only thence what you would say:
Then to be able to speak sense
Were an offence:
And 'twill thy passion tell the subtlest way,   45
Not to know what to say!

# APPENDIX OF POEMS

### Attributed to Carew and included in various Editions of his Poems.

## NOTE.

In the 1640 edition of Carew's poems two poems of which he was certainly not the author were included, namely Herrick's *Primrose* ('Ask me why I send you here') and his *Enquiry* ('Amongst the myrtles as I walked'). In the edition of 1642 was added Waller's address to the Lord Admiral, the Earl of Northumberland ('With joy like ours the Thracian youth invade"). Later editors have included the song from Jonson's *Volpone* ('Come, my Celia, let us prove') and Dr. Henry King's *Surrender* ('My once dear love, hapless that I no more'), and the same writer's lines *To his inconstant Mistress* ('But say, you very woman, why to me'), but in no case with any show of authority. None of the poems named is here reprinted.

The first and succeeding editions also include three poems by Shirley and one by Suckling, but as these appeared in Carew's works with considerable variations, they may possibly have been altered by him, and are therefore reproduced.

## THE HUE AND CRY.

*As printed in Shirley's Poems.*

In Love's name you are charged, oh, fly
And make a speedy hue and cry
After a face, which t'other day
Stole my wandering heart away.
To direct you, take in brief,                          5
These few marks to know the thief.
Her hair a net of beams would prove,
Strong enough to imprison Jove
Dress'd in his eagle's shape: her brow
Is a spacious field of snow:                           10
Her eyes so rich, so pure a grey,
Every look creates a day.
And if they close themselves (not when
The sun doth set) 'tis night again.
In her cheeks are to be seen                           15
Of flowers both the king and queen,
Thither by all the graces led,
And smiling in their nuptial bed;
On whom, like pretty nymphs, do wait,
Her twin-born lips, whose virgin state                 20
They do deplore themselves, nor miss
To blush, so often as they kiss,
Without a man. Beside the rest,
You shall know this felon best
By her tongue; for when your ear                       25
Once a harmony shall hear
So ravishing, you do not know
Whether you be in heaven or no,
That, that is she; oh straight surprise
And bring her unto Love's assize;                      30
But lose no time for fear that she
Ruin all mankind, like me,
Fate and philosophy control,
And leave the world without a soul.

## THE HUE AND CRY.

*As printed in Carew's Poems.*

In Love's name you are charged hereby
To make a speedy hue and cry
After a face, which, t'other day,
Stole my wandering heart away.
To direct you, these, in brief,                 5
Are ready marks to know the thief.
Her hair a net of beams would prove
Strong enough to captive Jove,
In his eagle's shape; her brow
Is a comely field of snow;                     10
Her eye so rich, so pure a grey,
Every beam creates a day:
And, if she but sleep (not when
The sun sets), 'tis night again.
In her cheeks are to be seen                   15
Of flowers both the king and queen,
Thither by the graces led,
And freshly laid in nuptial bed;
On whose lips like nymphs do wait,
Who deplore their virgin state:                20
Oft they blush, and blush for this,
That they one another kiss.
But observe, besides the rest,
You shall know this felon best
By her tongue; for if your ear                 25
Once a heavenly music hear,
Such as neither gods nor men,
But from that voice, shall hear again,
That, that is she. O! straight surprise,
And bring her unto Love's assize.              30
If you let her go, she may
Ante-date the latter day,
Fate and philosophy control,
And leave the world without a soul.

## THE HUE AND CRY.

*From Shirley's "Witty Fair One,"* 1628.

In Love's name you are charged hereby
To make a speedy hue and cry
After a face, which t'other day
Came and stole my heart away.
For your directions, in brief, 5
These are best marks to know the thief:
Her hair a net of beams would prove,
Strong enough to captive Jove,
Playing the eagle: her clear brow
Is a comely field of snow. 10
A sparkling eye, so pure a grey,
As when it shines it needs no day.
Ivory dwelleth on her nose;
Lilies married to the rose
Have made her cheek the nuptial bed; 15
Lips betray their virgins' weed,
As they only blush'd for this,
That they one another kiss.
But observe, beside the rest,
You shall know this felon best 20
By her tongue; for if your ear
Shall once a heavenly music hear,
Such as neither gods nor men
But from that voice shall hear again,
That, that is she: oh, take her t' ye, 25
None can rock heaven asleep but she.

## SONG.

### (*By Shirley.*)

WOULD you know what's soft?  I dare
Remit you to the down or air :
The stars we all acknowledge bright,
The snow too is exceeding white :
To please your scent 'twill not be hard          5
To present you bruised nard ;
And would you heavenly music hear
I'll call the orbs to take your ear,
If old Pythagoras sing true :
But ambrosia, heavenly dew                       10
Divinely must affect your taste
And nectar is your drink at last :
But would you have all these delights in one
Know but the fair Odelia and 'tis done.

*The same as printed in Carew's Poems.*

WOULD you know what's soft?  I dare
Not bring you to the down, or air ;
Nor to stars to show what's bright ;
Nor to snow to teach you white.

   Nor, if you would music hear,          5
Call the orbs to take your ear ;
Nor, to please your sense, bring forth
Bruised nard or what's more worth.

   Or, on food were your thoughts placed,
Bring you nectar for a taste :                   10
Would you have all these in one ?
Name my mistress, and 'tis done.

## TO HIS MISTRESS CONFINED.

### *Song (by Shirley).*

THINK not, my Phœbe, 'cause a cloud
Doth now thy heavenly beauty shroud,
  My wand'ring eye
Can stoop to common beauties of the sky.
 Rather be kind, and this eclipse    5
 Shall neither hinder eyes nor lips;
  For we shall meet
Within our hearts, and kiss, and none shall see't.

Nor can'st thou in thy prison be
Without some living sign of me;    10
  When thou dost spy
A sunbeam peep into thy room, 'tis I:
 For I am hid within that flame,
 And thus into thy chamber came,
  To let thee see    15
In what a martyrdom I burn for thee.

[*When thou dost touch thy lute, thou may'st
Think on my heart, on which thou play'st;
  When each sad tone
Upon the strings doth show my deeper groan:*   20
 *When thou dost please, they shall rebound
 With nimble airs, struck to the sound
  Of thy own voice;
O think, how much I tremble and rejoice!*]

There's no sad picture that doth dwell    25
Upon thy arras-wall, but well
  Resembles me;

  No matter though our years do not agree.
   Love can make old as well as Time ;
   And he that doth but twenty climb,  30
    If he will prove
  As true as I, shows four-score years in love.


## VARIATIONS IN CAREW'S VERSION.

l. 1. commences '*Oh*' and omits '*my.*'
l. 2. *silver brightness* for *heavenly beauty.*
l. 12. *the* for *thy.*
l. 13. *a* for *that.*
ll. 16—24. This stanza does not appear in Shirley's copy.
l. 28. *age* for *years.*
l. 31. *dare* for *will.*

## THE GUILTLESS INCONSTANT.

### (*By Suckling.*)

My first love, whom all beauties did adorn,
Firing my heart, suppress'd it with her scorn,
Since like to tinder in my breast it lies,
By every sparkle made a sacrifice.
Each wanton eye can kindle my desire,       5
And that is free to all which was entire.
Desiring more, by the desire I lost,
As those that in consumptions linger most ;
And now my wand'ring thoughts are not confined
Unto one woman, but to woman-kind.          10
This for her shape I love, that for her face,
This for her gesture, or some other grace ;
And where that none of all these things I find,
I choose her by the kernel, not the rind.
And so I hope, since my first hope is gone,  15
To find in many what I lost in one ;
And, like to merchants after some great loss,
Trade by retail, that cannot do in gross.

### VARIATIONS IN CAREW'S POEMS 1640.

Headed 'The Spark.'

l. 3. *Sunlike to tinder in my breast it lies.*
l. 5. *Now kindles.*
l. 7. *By thee desire I got.*
l. 8. *Hunger most.*
l. 11. *Shape of love.*
l. 13. *Where I none of these do use to find.*
l. 14. *I choose thereby.*
l. 15. *Hopes are gone.*
l. 18. *Cannot now.*

The fault is her's, that made me go astray:
He needs must wander that hath lost his way.   20
Guiltless I am: she doth this change provoke,
And made that charcoal which to her was oak.
And as a looking-glass from the aspect,
Whilst it is whole, doth but one face reflect,
But, being crack'd or broken, there are grown   25
Many less faces, where there was but one;
So Love unto my heart did first prefer
Her image, and there placed none but her:
But since 'twas broke, and martyr'd by her scorn,
Many less faces in her place are born.   30

> l. 21. *She did.*
> l. 25. *Shown* for *grown.*
> l. 28. *Planted* for *placed*
> l. 30. *In her face are born.*

*The following Couplet is added:*

Thus, like to tinder, am I prone to catch
Each falling sparkle, fit for any match.

# CAREW'S MASQUE.

# COELVM BRITANNICVM.

## A MASQVE,

AT WHITE-HALL IN THE BANQUETTING-HOUSE,

On Shrove-Tuesday Night, the 18 of February

1633.

*Non habeo ingenium; Cæsar sed jussit; habebo:*
*Cur me posse negem, posse quod ille putat?*

# THE MASQUE:

## COELUM BRITANNICUM.

### The Description of the Scene.

THE first thing that presented itself to the sight, was a rich ornament, that enclosed the scene; in the upper part of which were great branches of foliage, growing out of leaves and husks, with a coronice at the top; and in the midst was placed a large compartment, composed of grotesque work, wherein were harpies with wings and lions' claws, and their hinder parts converted into leaves and branches: over all was a broken frontispiece, wrought with scrolls and mask-heads of children; and within this a table, adorned with a lesser compartment, with this inscription, COELUM BRITANNICUM. The two sides of this ornament were thus ordered: First, from the ground arose a square basement, and on the plinth stood a great vase of gold, richly enchased, and beautified with sculptures of great relief, with fruitages hanging from the upper part: at the foot of this sat two youths, naked, in their natural colours; each of these with one arm supported the vase, on the cover of which stood two young women, in draperies, arm in arm: the one figuring the Glory of Princes, and the other Mansuetude: their other arms bore up an oval, in which, to the King's Majesty, was this impress—a lion, with an imperial crown on his head: the word, *Animum sub pectore forti*. On the other side was the like composition, but the design of the figures varied; and in the oval on the top, being borne up by Nobility and Fecundity, was this impress, to the Queen's Majesty, a lily growing with branches and leaves, and three lesser lilies springing out of the stem; the word, *Semper inclita Virtus*. All this ornament was heightened with gold, and for the invention and various composition was the newest and most gracious that hath been done in this place.

The curtain was watchet and a pale yellow in panes; which, flying up on the sudden, discovered the scene, representing old arches, old palaces, decayed walls, parts of temples, theatres, basilicas, and thermæ, with confused heaps of broken columns, bases, coronices, and statues, lying as under ground; and altogether resembling the ruins of some great city of the ancient Romans or civilized Britons. This strange prospect detained the eyes of the spectators some time, when, to a loud music, Mercury descends; on the upper part of his chariot stands a cock, in action of crowing. His habit was a coat of flame colour, girt to him, and a white mantle trimmed with gold and silver; upon his head a wreath, with small falls of white feathers, a caduceus

in his hand, and wings at his heels. Being come to
the ground, he dismounts, and goes up to the state.

*Mercury.*

FROM the high senate of the gods, to you,
Bright glorious twins of love and majesty,
Before whose throne three warlike nations bend
Their willing knees: on whose imperial brows
The regal circle prints no awful frowns
To fright your subjects, but whose calmer eyes
Shed joy and safety on their melting hearts,
That flow with cheerful loyal reverence,
Come I, Cyllenius, Jove's ambassador;
Not, as of old, to whisper amorous tales
Of wanton love into the glowing ear
Of some choice beauty in this numerous train:
Those days are fled, the rebel flame is quench'd
In heavenly breasts; the gods have sworn by Styx,
Never to tempt yielding mortality
To loose embraces. Your exemplar life
Hath not alone transfused a zealous heat
Of imitation through your virtuous court,
By whose bright blaze your palace is become
The envy'd pattern of this under-world,
But the aspiring flame hath kindled heaven;
Th' immortal bosoms burn with emulous fires,
Love rivals your great virtues, royal sir,
And Juno, madam, your attractive graces.
He his wild lusts, her raging jealousies
She lays aside, and through th' Olympic hall,

As yours doth here, their great example spreads.
And though of old, when youthful blood conspired
With his new empire, prone to heats of lust,
He acted incests, rapes, adulteries,
On earthly beauties which his raging Queen,
Swoln with revengeful fury, turn'd to beasts,
And in despite he re-transform'd to stars,
Till he had fill'd the crowded firmament
With his loose strumpets, and their spurious race,
Where the eternal records of his shame
Shine to the world in flaming characters;
When in the crystal mirror of your reign
He view'd himself, he found his loathsome stains:
And now, to expiate the infectious guilt
Of those detested luxuries, he'll chase
Th' infamous lights from their usurped sphere,
And drown in the Lethæan flood their curst
Both names and memories; in whose vacant rooms
First you succeed, and of the wheeling orb
In the most eminent and conspicuous point,
With dazzling beams and spreading magnitude,
Shine the bright Pole-star of this hemisphere.
Next, by your side, in a triumphant chair,
And crown'd with Ariadne's diadem,
Sits the fair consort of your heart and throne.
Diffused about you, with that share of light,
As they of virtue have derived from you,
He'll fix this noble train, of either sex;
So to the British stars this lower globe
Shall owe its light, and they alone dispense
To the world a pure refined influence.

Enter Momus, attired in a long darkish robe, all
wrought over with poniards, serpents' tongues,
eyes, and ears; his beard and hair parti-coloured,
and upon his head a wreath stuck with feathers,
and a porcupine in the forepart.

*Momus.*

By your leave, Mortals. Good-den, Cousin
Hermes! your pardon, good my Lord Ambassador.
I found the tables of your arms and titles in every
inn betwixt this and Olympus, where your present
expedition is registered your nine thousandth nine
hundred ninety-ninth Legation. I cannot reach the
policy why your master breeds so few statesmen; it
suits not with his dignity that in the whole empyræum
there should not be a god fit to send on these honour-
able errands but yourself, who are not yet so careful
of his honour as your own, as might become your
quality, when you are itinerant: the hosts upon the
high-way cry out with open mouth upon you, for
supporting pilfery in your train; which, though as you
are the god of petty larceny, you might protect, yet
you know it is directly against the new orders, and
opposes the reformation in diameter.

*Mercury.*—Peace, railer! bridle your licentious
tongue,
And let this presence teach you modesty.

*Momus.*—Let it, if it can; in the mean time I will
acquaint it with my condition. Know, gay people,
that though your poets, who enjoy by patent a par-

ticular privilege to draw down any of the deities, from Twelfth-night till Shrove-Tuesday, at what time there is annually a most familiar intercourse between the two courts, have as yet never invited me to these solemnities; yet it shall appear by my intrusion this night, that I am a very considerable person upon these occasions, and may most properly assist at such entertainments. My name is Momus-ap-Somnus-ap-Erebus-ap-Chaos-ap-Demogorgon-ap-Eternity. My offices and titles are, the supreme Theomastix, Hypercritic of manners, Protonotary of abuses, Arch-Informer, Dilator-General, Universal Calumniator, Eternal Plaintiff, and perpetual Foreman of the Grand Inquest. My privileges are an ubiquitary, circumambulatory, speculatory, interrogatory, redargutory immunity over all the privy lodgings, behind hangings, doors, curtains, through key-holes, chinks, windows, about all venereal lobbies, sconces, or redoubts: though it be to the surprise of a *perdu* page or chambermaid; in and at all Courts of civil and criminal judicature, all counsels, consultations, and Parliamentary assemblies, where, though I am but a Wool-sack god, and have no vote in the sanction of new laws, I have yet a prerogative of wresting the old to any whatsoever interpretation, whether it be to the behoof or prejudice of Jupiter his crown and dignity, for or against the rights of either house of patrician or plebeian gods. My natural qualities are to make Jove frown, Juno pout, Mars chafe, Venus blush, Vulcan glow, Saturn quake, Cynthia pale, Phœbus hide his face, and Mercury here take his heels. My recreations are witty mischiefs, as when Saturn gelt his father; the smith caught his wife and her bravo in a net of cobweb-iron; and Hebe, through the lubricity of the pavement tumbling over the half-pace, presented the emblem of the forked tree, and discovered to the tanned Ethiops the snowy cliffs of Culabria with the Grotta of Puteolum. But that you may arrive at the perfect knowledge of me by the familiar illustration of a bird of mine own feather, old Peter Aretine, who reduced all the sceptres and mitres of that age tributary to his wit, was my parallel; and Frank Rabelais sucked much of my milk too; but your modern French hospital of oratory is mere counterfeit, an arrant mountebank; for, though fearing no other tortures than his sciatica, he discourses of kings and queens with as little reverence as of grooms and chambermaids, yet he wants their fang-teeth and scorpion's tail: I mean that fellow who, to add to his stature thinks it a greater grace to dance on his tiptoes like a dog in a doublet, than to walk like other men on the soles of his feet.

*Mercury.*—No more, impertinent trifler! you disturb
The great affair with your rude scurrilous chat:
What doth the knowledge of your abject state
Concern Jove's solemn message?

*Momus.*—Sir, by your favour, though you have a more especial commission of employment from Jupiter, and a larger entertainment from his Ex-

chequer, yet as a free-born god I have the liberty
to travel at mine own charges, without your pass or
countenance legacine; and that it may appear a
sedulous acute observer may know as much as a dull
phlegmatic ambassador, and wears a treble key to
unlock the mysterious cyphers of your dark secrecies,
I will discourse the politic state of Heaven to this
trim audience.—

> At this the scene changeth, and in the heaven is discovered a sphere, with stars placed in their several images, borne up by a huge naked figure (only a piece of drapery hanging over his thigh), kneeling and bowing forwards, as if the great weight lying on his shoulders oppressed him; upon his head a crown: by all which he might easily be known to be Atlas.

—You shall understand that Jupiter, upon the inspection of I know not what virtuous precedents, extant, as they say, here in this Court (but, as I more probably guess, out of the consideration of the decay of his natural abilities), hath before a frequent convocation of the superlunary peers in a solemn oration recanted, disclaimed, and utterly renounced, all the lascivious extravagancies and riotous enormities of his forepast licentious life; and taken his oath on Juno's Breviary, religiously kissing the two-leaved Book, never to stretch his limbs more betwixt adulterous sheets: and hath with pathetical remonstrances exhorted, and under strict penalties enjoined, a respective conformity in the several subordinate deities. And because the libertines of antiquity, the ribald poets, to perpetuate the memory and example of their triumphs over chastity to all future imitation, have in their immortal songs celebrated the martyrdom of those strumpets under the persecution of the wives, and devolved to posterity the pedigrees of their whores, bawds, and bastards; it is therefore by the authority aforesaid enacted, that this whole army of constellations be immediately disbanded and cashiered, so to remove all imputation of impiety from the celestial spirits, and all lustful influences upon terrestrial bodies; and, consequently, that there be an inquisition erected to expunge in the ancient, and suppress in the modern and succeeding poems and pamphlets, all past, present, and future mention of those abjured heresies, and to take particular notice of all ensuing incontinencies, and punish them in their high Commission Court. Am not I in election to be a tall statesman, think you, that can repeat a passage at a council-table thus punctually?

*Mercury.*—I shun in vain the importunity
With which this snarler vexeth all the gods;
Jove cannot 'scape him. Well, what else from
heaven?

*Momus.*—Heaven! Heaven is no more the place it was: a cloister of Carthusians, a monastery of converted gods; Jove is grown old and fearful, apprehends a subversion of his empire, and doubts lest Fate should introduce a legal succession in the legitimate heir, by repossessing the Titanian line: and hence springs all this innovation. We have had new orders read in the presence chamber by the Vi'-President of Parnassus, too strict to be observed long. Monopolies are called in, sophistication of wares punished, and rates imposed on commodities. Injunctions are gone out to the nectar brewers, for the purging of the heavenly beverage of a narcotic weed which hath rendered the ideas confused in the divine intellects, and reducing it to the composition used in Saturn's reign. Edicts are made for the restoring of decayed house-keeping, prohibiting the repair of families to the metropolis; but this did endanger an Amazonian mutiny, till the females put on a more masculine resolution of soliciting businesses in their own persons, and leaving their husbands at home for stallions of hospitality. Bacchus hath commanded all taverns to be shut, and no liquor drawn after ten at night. Cupid must go no more so scandalously naked, but is enjoined to make him breeches, though of his mother's petticoats. Ganymede is forbidden the bed-chamber, and must only minister in public. The gods must keep no pages, nor grooms of their chamber, under the age of 25, and those provided of a competent stock of beard. Pan may not pipe, nor Proteus juggle, but by especial permission. Vulcan was brought to an *Ore-tenus*, and fined, for driving in a plate of iron into one of the Sun's chariot-wheels, and frost-nailing his horses upon the fifth of November last, for breach of a penal Statute prohibiting work upon holidays, that being

the annual celebration of the Gigantomachy. In
brief, the whole state of the Hierarchy suffers a total
reformation, especially in the point of reciprocation
of conjugal affection. Venus hath confessed all her
adulteries, and is received to grace by her husband,
who, conscious of the great disparity betwixt her
perfections and his deformities, allows those levities
as an equal counterpoise; but it is the prettiest specta-
cle to see her stroking with her ivory hand his collied
cheeks, and with her snowy fingers combing his
sooty beard. Jupiter too begins to learn to lead his
own wife; I left him practising in the milky way;
and there is no doubt of an universal obedience,
where the law-giver himself in his own person
observes his decrees so punctually: who, besides, to
eternize the memory of that great example of matri-
monial union which he derives from hence, hath on
his bed-chamber door and ceiling, fretted with stars
in capital letters, engraven the inscription of CARLO-
MARIA. This is as much, I am sure, as either
your knowledge or instructions can direct you to,
which I, having in a blunt round tale, without state-
formality, politic inferences, or suspected rhetorical
elegancies, already delivered, you may now dexter-
ously proceed to the second part of your charge,
which is the raking of yon heavenly sparks up in the
embers, or reducing the etherial lights to their
primitive opacity and gross dark substance; they are
all unriveted from the sphere, and hang loose in
their sockets, where they but attend the waving of
your Caduce, and immediately they re-invest their

pristine shapes, and appear before you in their own natural deformities.

*Mercury.*—Momus, thou shalt prevail, for since
    thy bold
Intrusion hath inverted my resolves,
I must obey necessity, and thus turn
My face, to breathe the Thunderer's just decree
'Gainst this adulterate sphere, which first I purge
Of loathsome monsters and mis-shapen forms:
Down from her azure concave thus I charm
The Lyrnæan Hydra, the rough unlick'd Bear,
The watchful Dragon, the storm-boding Whale,
The Centaur, the horn'd Goat-fish Capricorn,
The Snake-head Gorgon, and fierce Sagittar.
Divested of your gorgeous starry robes,
Fall from the circling orb! and e'er you suck
Fresh venom in, measure this happy earth:
Then to the fens, caves, forests, deserts, seas,
Fly, and resume your native qualities!

*They dance, in those monstrous shapes, the first Antimasque, of natural deformity.*

*Momus.*—Are not these fine companions, trim play-fellows for the deities? Yet these and their fellows have made up all our conversation for some thousands of years. Do not you, fair ladies, acknowledge yourselves deeply engaged now to those poets, your servants, that, in the height of commendation, have raised your beauties to a parallel with such exact proportions or at least ranked you in their spruce society? Hath not the consideration of these inhabitants rather frighted your thoughts utterly from the contemplation of the place? But now that those heavenly mansions are to be void, you that shall hereafter be found unlodged will become inexcusable; especially since virtue alone shall be sufficient title, fine, and rent: yet if there be a lady, not competently stocked that way, she shall not on the instant utterly despair, if she carry a sufficient pawn of handsomeness; for however the letter of the law runs, Jupiter, notwithstanding his age and present austerity, will never refuse to stamp beauty, and make it current with his own impression; but to such as are destitute of both, I can afford but small encouragement. Proceed, cousin Mercury; what follows?

*Merc.*—Look up, and mark where the bright zodiac
Hangs like a belt about the breast of heaven;
On the right shoulder, like a flaming jewel,
His shell with nine rich topazes adorn'd,
Lord of this tropic, sits the scalding Crab:
He, when the Sun gallops in full career
His annual race, his ghastly claws uprear'd,
Frights at the confines of the torrid zone,
The fiery team, and proudly stops their course,
Making a solstice, till the fierce steeds learn
His backward paces, and so retrograde
Post down-hill to th' opposed Capricorn.
Thus I depose him from his haughty throne:
Drop from the sky into the briny flood;
There teach thy motion to the ebbing sea!
But let those fires that beautified thy shell

Take human shapes, and the disorder show
Of thy regressive paces here below.

*The second Antimasque is danced in retrograde paces,
expressing obliquity in motion.*

*Momus.*—This Crab, I confess, did ill become the heavens; but there is another that more infests the earth, and makes such a solstice in the politer arts and sciences, as they have not been observed for many ages to have made any sensible advance. Could you but lead the learned squadrons with a masculine resolution past this point of retrogradation, it were a benefit to mankind, worthy the power of a god, and to be paid with altars; but that not being the work of this night, you may pursue your purposes. What now succeeds?

*Mercury.*—Vice that, unbodied, in the appetite
Erects his throne, hath yet in bestial shapes,
Branded by Nature with the character
And distinct stamp of some peculiar ill,
Mounted the sky, and fix'd his trophies there:
As fawning flattery in the little dog,
I' th' bigger, churlish murmur; cowardice
I' th' timorous hare; ambition in the eagle;
Rapine and avarice in th' advent'rous ship
That sail'd to Colchis for the golden fleece.
Drunken distemper in the goblet flows;
I' th' Dart and Scorpion, biting calumny;
In Hercules and the Lion, furious rage;
Vain ostentation in Cassiope:

All these I to eternal exile doom,
But to this place their emblem'd vices summon,
Clad in those proper figures, by which best
Their incorporeal nature is express'd.

*The third Antimasque is danced of these several Vices, expressing the deviation from Virtue.*

*Momus.*—From henceforth it shall be no more said in the proverb, when you would express a riotous assembly, that hell, but heaven, is broke loose. This was an arrant Gaol-delivery; all the prisons of your great cities could not have vomited more corrupt matter; but, Cousin Cylleneus, in my judgment it is not safe that these infectious persons should wander here, to the hazard of this island; they threatened less danger when they were nailed to the firmament. I should conceive it a very discreet course, since they are provided of a tall vessel of their own, ready rigged, to embark them all together in that good ship called the Argo, and send them to the plantation in New England, which hath purged more virulent humours from the politic body, than Guiacum and all the West-Indian drugs have from the natural bodies of this kingdom. Can you devise how to dispose them better?

*Mercury.*—They cannot breathe this pure and
    temperate air,
Where Virtue lives; but will, with hasty flight,
'Mongst fogs and vapours, seek unsound abodes.
Fly after them, from your usurped seats,
You foul remainders of that viperous brood!

Let not a star of the luxurious race
With his loose blaze stain the sky's crystal face.

*All the Stars are quenched, and the Sphere darkened.*

Before the entry of every Antimasque, the stars in those figures in the sphere which they were to represent, were extinct; so as, by the end of the Antimasques, in the sphere no more stars were seen.

*Momus.*—Here is a total eclipse of the eighth sphere, which neither Booker, Allestre, nor any of your prognosticators, no, nor their great master, Tycho, were aware of; but yet, in my opinion, there were some innocent, and some generous constellations, that might have been reserved for noble uses; as the Scales and Sword to adorn the statue of Justice, since she resides here on earth only in picture and effigy. The Eagle had been a fit present for the Germans, in regard their bird hath mew'd most of her feathers lately. The Dolphin, too, had been most welcome to the French; and then, had you but clapt Perseus on his Pegasus, brandishing his sword, the Dragon yawning on his back under the horse's feet, with Python's[1] dart through his throat, there had been a divine St. George for this nation! but since you have improvidently shuffled them altogether, it now rests only that we provide an immediate succession; and to that purpose I will instantly proclaim a free election.

[1] Python. The old copy has Pytheus.

O yes, O yes, O yes!
By the Father of the gods,
and the King of Men.

Whereas we having observed a very commendable practice taken into frequent use by the princes of these latter ages, of perpetuating the memory of their famous enterprises, sieges, battles, victories, in picture, sculpture, tapestry, embroideries, and other manufactures, wherewith they have embellished their public palaces, and taken into our more distinct and serious consideration the particular Christmas hanging of the Guard-Chamber of this Court, wherein the naval victory of '88 is, to the eternal glory of this nation, exactly delineated; and whereas we likewise, out of a prophetical imitation of this so laudable custom, did, for many thousand years before, adorn and beautify the eighth room of our celestial mansion, commonly called the Star-Chamber, with the military adventures, stratagems, achievements, feats, and defeats, performed in our own person, whilst yet our standard was erected, and we a combatant in the amorous warfare: It hath, notwithstanding, after mature deliberation and long debate, held first in our own inscrutable bosom, and afterwards communicated with our Privy Council, seemed meet to our omnipotency, for causes to our self best known, to unfurnish and dis-array our foresaid Star-Chamber of all those ancient constellations which have for so many ages been sufficiently notorious, and to admit into their vacant places such persons only as shall be qualified, with exemplar virtue and eminent desert, there to shine in indelible characters of glory to all posterity. It is therefore our divine will and pleasure, voluntarily, and out of our own free and proper motion, mere grace and special favour, by these presents, to specify and declare to all our loving people, that it shall be lawful for any person whatsoever, that conceiveth him or her self to be really endued with any heroical virtue or transcendent merit, worthy so high a calling and dignity, to bring their several pleas and pretences before our right-trusty and well-beloved Cousin and Counsellor, Don Mercury and god Momus, &c., our peculiar delegates for that affair; upon whom we have transferr'd an absolute power to conlude and determine, without appeal or revocation, accordingly as to their wisdoms it shall in such cases appear behoveful and expedient. Given at our palace in Olympus the first day of the first month, in the first year of the Reformation.

Plutus enters, an old man full of wrinkles, a bald head, a thin white beard, spectacles on his nose, with a bunched back, and attired in a robe of cloth of gold.

*Plutus appears.*

*Mercury.*—Who's this appears?

*Momus.*—This is a subterranean fiend, Plutus, in this dialect term'd Riches, or the god of gold; a poison hid by Providence, in the bottom of seas[1] and

---

[1] The 1640 edition inserts *the* before *seas*.

navel of the earth, from man's discovery; where, if the seeds began to sprout above-ground, the excrescence was carefully guarded by Dragons; yet at last, by human curiosity, brought to light to their own destruction, this being the true Pandora's box, whence issued all those mischiefs that now fill the universe.

*Plutus.*—That I prevent the message of the gods
Thus with my haste, and not attend their summons,
Which ought in justice call me to the place
I now require of right, is not alone
To show the just precedence that I hold
Before all earthly, next th' immortal, powers;
But to exclude the hope of partial grace
In all pretenders, who, since I descend
To equal trial, must by my example,
Waiving your favour, claim by sole desert.
If Virtue must inherit, she's my slave;
I lead her captive in a golden chain,
About the world; she takes her form and being
From my creation; and those barren seeds
That drop from Heaven, if I not cherish them
With my distilling dews and fotive heat,
They know no vegetation; but, exposed
To blasting winds of freezing poverty,
Or not shoot forth at all, or, budding, wither.
Should I proclaim the daily sacrifice
Brought to my temples by the toiling rout,
Not of the fat and gore of abject beasts
But human sweat and blood pour'd on my altars,
I might provoke the envy of the gods.
Turn but your eyes, and mark the busy world,

Climbing steep mountains for the sparkling stone,
Piercing the centre for the shining ore,
And th' ocean's bosom to rake pearly sands;
Crossing the torrid and the frozen zones,
'Midst rocks and swallowing gulfs, for gainful trade,
And through opposing swords, fire, murd'ring cannon,
Scaling the walled towns for precious spoils.
Plant, in the passage to your heavenly seats,
These horrid dangers, and then see who dares
Advance his desperate foot; yet am I sought,
And oft in vain, through these and greater hazards:
I could discover how your deities
Are for my sake slighted, despised, abused;
Your temples, shrines, altars, and images,
Uncover'd, rifled, robb'd and disarray'd
By sacrilegious hands; yet is this treasure
To th' golden mountain, where I sit adored,
With superstitious solemn rites convey'd,
And becomes sacred there; the sordid wretch
Not daring touch the consecrated ore,
Or with profane hands lessen the bright heap:
But this might draw your anger down on mortals,
For rend'ring me the homage due to you;
Yet what is said may well express my power,
Too great for earth, and only fit for Heaven.

  Now, for your pastime, view the naked root
Which, in the dirty earth and base mould drown'd,
Sends forth this precious plant and golden fruit.
You lusty swains, that to your grazing flocks
Pipe amorous roundelays; you toiling hinds,
That barb the fields, and to your merry teams

Whistle your passions; and you mining moles,
That in the bowels of your mother earth
Dwell, the eternal burden of her womb,
Cease from your labours, when Wealth bids you play,
Sing, dance, and keep a cheerful holiday.

*They dance the fourth Antimasque, consisting of
Country people, music, and measures.*

*Mercury.*—Plutus, the gods know and confess your power,
Which feeble virtue seldom can resist;
Stronger than towers of brass or chastity:
Jove knew you when he courted Danae,
And Cupid wears you on that arrow's head
That still prevails. But the gods keep their thrones
To install Virtue, not her enemies.
They dread thy force, which even themselves have felt:
Witness Mount Ida, where the martial maid
And frowning Juno did to mortal eyes
Naked for gold their sacred bodies show,
Therefore for ever be from heaven banish'd:
But since with toil from undiscover'd worlds
Thou art brought hither, where thou first did'st breathe
The thirst of empire into regal breasts,
And frightedst quiet Peace from her meek throne,
Filling the world with tumult, blood, and war;
Follow the camps of the contentious earth,
And be the conqueror's slave: but he that can
Or conquer thee, or give thee virtue's stamp,
Shall shine in heaven a pure immortal lamp.

*Momus.*—Nay, stay, and take my benediction along

with you! I could, being here a co-judge, like
others in my place, now that you are condemned,
either rail at you, or break jests upon you; but I
rather choose to loose a word of good counsel, and
entreat you to be more careful in your choice of
company; for you are always found either with
misers, that not use you at all, or with fools, that
know not how to use you well. Be not hereafter so
reserved and coy to men of worth and parts, and so
you shall gain such credit, as at the next Sessions you
may be heard with better success. But till you are
thus reformed, I pronounce this positive sentence,
That wheresoever you shall choose to abide, your
society shall add no credit or reputation to the party,
nor your discontinuance or total absence be matter of
disparagement to any man; and whosoever shall
hold a contrary estimation of you, shall be condemned
to wear perpetual motley, unless he recant his
opinion. Now you may void the Court.

> Penia enters, a woman of pale colour, large brims
> of a hat upon her head, through which her
> hair started up like a fury; her robe was of a
> dark colour, full of patches; about one of her
> hands was tied a chain of iron, to which was
> fastened a weighty stone, which she bore up
> under her arm.

### *Penia enters.*

*Mercury.*—What creature's this?
*Momus.*—The Antipodes to the other: they move

like two buckets, or as two nails drive out one
another.  If riches depart, poverty will enter.

*Poverty.*—I nothing doubt, great and immortal
    Powers,
But that the place your wisdom hath denied
My foe, your justice will confer on me ;
Since that which renders him incapable
Proves a strong plea for me.  I could pretend,
Even in these rags, a larger sovereignty
Than gaudy Wealth in all his pomp can boast ;
For mark how few they are that share the world ;
The numerous armies, and the swarming ants
That fight and toil for them, are all my subjects,
They take my wages, wear my livery :
Invention too and Wit are both my creatures,
And the whole race of Virtue is my offspring :
As many mischiefs issue from my womb,
And those as mighty, as proceed from gold.
Oft o'er his throne I wave my awful sceptre,
And in the bowels of his state command,
When, midst his heaps of coin and hills of gold,
I pine and starve the avaricious fool.
But I decline those titles, and lay claim
To heaven by right of divine contemplation :
She is my darling, I, in my soft lap,
Free from disturbing cares, bargains, accounts,
Leases, rents, stewards, and the fear of thieves
That vex the rich, nurse her in calm repose,
And with her all the virtues speculative,
Which but with me find no secure retreat.
For entertainment of this hour, I'll call

A race of people to this place, that live
At Nature's charge, and not importune heaven
To chain the winds up, or keep back the storms,
To stay the thunder, or forbid the hail
To thresh the unreap'd ear, but to all weathers,
Both chilling frost and scalding sun, expose
Their equal face. Come forth, my swarthy train!
In this fair circle dance, and as you move,
Mark and foretell happy events of love.

*They dance the fifth* Antimasque, *of Gipsies.*

*Momus.*—I cannot but wonder, that your perpetual conversation with poets and philosophers hath furnished you with no more logic, or that you should think to impose upon us so gross an inference, as because Plutus and you are contrary, therefore whatsoever is denied of the one must be true of the other; as if it should follow of necessity, because he is not Jupiter, you are. No, I give you to know, I am better versed in cavils with the gods than to swallow such a fallacy; for though you two cannot be together in one place, yet there are many places that may be without you both, and such is heaven, where neither of you are likely to arrive: therefore let me advise you to marry yourself to Content, and beget sage apophthegms and goodly moral sentences, in dispraise of riches, and contempt of the world.

*Mercury.*—Thou dost presume too much, poor needy wretch,
To claim a station in the firmament,
Because thy humble cottage or thy tub

Nurses some lazy or pedantic virtue,
In the cheap sun-shine or by shady springs,
With roots and pot-herbs ; where thy rigid hand,
Tearing those human passions from the mind,
Upon whose stocks fair blooming virtues flourish,
Degradeth Nature, and benumbeth sense,
And Gorgon-like, turns active men to stone.
We not require the dull society
Of your necessitated temperance,
Or that unnatural stupidity
That knows nor joy nor sorrow ; nor your forced
Falsely exalted, passive fortitude
Above the active.  This low abject brood,
That fix their seats in mediocrity,
Become your servile minds ; but we advance
Such virtues only as admit excess,
Brave bounteous acts, regal magnificence,
All-seeing prudence, magnanimity
That knows no bound, and that heroic virtue
For which antiquity hath left no name,
But patterns only, such as Hercules,
Achilles, Theseus.  Back to thy loathed cell !
And when thou seest the new enlighten'd sphere,
Study to know but what those worthies were.

>Tyche enters : her head bald behind, and one great lock before ; wings at her shoulders, and in her hand a wheel ; her upper parts naked, and the skirt of her garment wrought all over with crowns, sceptres, books, and such other things as express both her greatest and smallest gifts.

>>l. 3.   Ed. 1640, *right hand*.

*Momus.*—See where Dame Fortune comes; you may know her by her wheel, and that veil over eyes, with which she hopes, like a sealed pigeon, to mount above the clouds and perch in the eighth sphere. Listen! she begins.

*Fortune.*—I come not here, you gods, to plead the right
By which antiquity assign'd my deity,
Though no peculiar station 'mongst the stars,
Yet general power to rule their influence;
Or boast the title of omnipotent,
Ascribed me then, by which I rivall'd Jove,
Since you have cancell'd all those old records:
But, confident in my good cause and merit,
Claim a succession in the vacant orb.
For since Astræa fled to heaven, I sit
Her deputy on earth; I hold her scales,
And weigh men's fates out, who have made me blind,
Because themselves want eyes to see my causes;
Call me inconstant, 'cause my works surpass
The shallow fathom of their human reason;
Yet here, like blinded Justice, I dispense
With my impartial hands their constant lots:
And if desertless impious men engross
My best rewards, the fault is yours, you gods,
That scant your graces to mortality,
And, niggards of your good, scarce spare the world
One virtuous for a thousand wicked men.
It is no error to confer dignity,
But to bestow it on a vicious man;

l. 2. The 1640 edition inserts *her* before *eyes*.

I gave the dignity, but you made the vice :
Make you men good, and I'll make good men happy.
That Plutus is refused, dismays me not ;
He is my drudge, and the external pomp
In which he decks the world proceeds from me,
Not him ; like Harmony, that not resides
In strings or notes, but in the hand and voice.
The revolutions of empires, states,
Sceptres and crowns, are but my game and sport,
Which as they hang on the events of war,
So those depend upon my turning wheel.
  You warlike squadrons, who, in battles join'd,
Dispute the right of kings, which I decide,
Present the model of that martial frame,
By which, when crowns are staked, I rule the game !

*They dance the sixth Antimasque, being the representation of a battle.*

  *Momus.*—Madam, I should censure you, *pro falso clamore*,—for preferring a scandalous cross-bill of recrimination against the gods ; but your blindness shall excuse you. Alas ! what would it advantage you, if virtue were as universal as vice is ? It would only follow that, as the world now exclaims upon you for exalting the vicious, it would then rail as fast at you for depressing the virtuous ; so they would still keep their tune, though you changed their ditty.

  *Mercury.*—The mists in which future events are
      wrapp'd,
That oft succeed beside the purposes
Of him that works (his dull eyes not discerning

The first great cause), offer'd thy clouded shape
To his enquiring search; so in the dark
The groping world first found thy deity,
And gave thee rule over contingencies,
Which to the piercing eye of Providence
Being fixed and certain, where past and to-come
Are always present, thou dost disappear,
Losest thy being, and art not all.
Be thou then only a deluding phantom,
At best a blind guide, leading blinder fools:
Who, would they but survey their mutual wants,
And help each other, there were left no room
For thy vain aid. Wisdom, whose strong-built plots
Leave nought to hazard, mocks thy futile power;
Industrious Labour drags thee by the locks,
Bound to his toiling car, and, not attending
Till thou dispense, reaches his own reward;
Only the lazy sluggard yawning lies
Before thy threshold, gaping for thy dole,
And licks the easy hand that feeds his sloth;
The shallow, rash, and unadvised man
Makes thee his stale, disburdens all the follies
Of his mis-guided actions on thy shoulders.
Vanish from hence, and seek those idiots out
That thy fantastic god-head hath allow'd,
And rule that giddy superstitious crowd.

> Hedone, Pleasure, a young woman with a smiling face, in a light lascivious habit, adorned with silver and gold; her temples crowned with a garland of roses, and over that a rainbow circling her head down to her shoulders.

*Hedone enters.*

*Mercury.*—What wanton's this?

*Momus.*—This is the sprightly Lady Hedone, a merry gamester: this people call her Pleasure.

*Pleasure.*—The reasons, equal judges, here alleged
By the dismiss'd pretenders, all concur
To strengthen my just title to the sphere.
Honour or wealth, or the contempt of both,
Have in themselves no simple real good,
But as they are the means to purchase Pleasure,
The paths that lead to my delicious palace.
They for my sake, I for mine own, am prized.
Beyond me nothing is; I am the goal,
The journey's end, to which the sweating world
And wearied Nature travels. For this, the best
And wisest sect of all philosophers
Made me the seat of supreme happiness;
And though some, more austere, upon my ruins
Did, to the prejudice of Nature, raise
Some petty low-built virtues, 'twas because
They wanted wings to reach my soaring pitch.
Had they been princes born, themselves had proved
Of all mankind the most luxurious;
For those delights, which to their low condition
Were obvious, they with greedy appetite
Suck'd and devour'd: from offices of state,
From cares of family, children, wife, hopes, fears,
Retired, the churlish Cynic in his tub
Enjoy'd those pleasures which his tongue defamed.
Nor am I rank'd 'mongst the superfluous goods;

My necessary offices preserve
Each single man, and propagate the kind.
Then am I universal, as the light,
Or common air we breathe; and since I am
The general desire of all mankind,
Civil felicity must reside in me.
Tell me what rate my choicest pleasures bear
When, for the short delight of a poor draught
Of cheap cold water, great Lysimachus
Rendered himself slave to the Scythians?
Should I the curious structure of my seats,
The art and beauty of my several objects,
Rehearse at large, your bounties would reserve
For every sense a proper constellation;
But I present their persons to your eyes;
  Come forth, my subtle organs of delight!
With changing figures please the curious eye,
And charm the ear with moving harmony.

*They dance the seventh Antimasque, of the five Senses.*

  *Mercury.*—Bewitching Syren, gilded rottenness!
Thou hast with cunning artifice display'd
Th' enamel'd outside and the honied verge
Of the fair cup, where deadly poison lurks:
Within, a thousand sorrows dance the round,
And like a shell, pain circles thee without;
Grief is the shadow waiting on thy steps,
Which, as thy joys 'gin tow'rds their west decline,
Doth to a giant's spreading form extend
Thy dwarfish stature. Thou thyself art Pain,

Greedy, intense desire, and the keen edge
Of thy fierce appetite oft strangles thee,
And cuts thy slender thread; but still the terror
And apprehension of thy hasty end
Mingles with gall thy most refined sweets:
Yet thy Circean charms transform the world.
Captains, that have resisted war and death,
Nations, that over fortune have triumph'd,
Are by thy magic made effeminate:
Empires, that knew no limit but the Poles,
Have in thy wanton lap melted away.
Thou wert the author of the first excess
That drew this reformation on the gods.
Can'st thou then dream, those powers that from
    heaven have
Banish'd th' effect, will there enthrone the cause?
To thy voluptuous den, fly, Witch, from hence!
There dwell, for ever drown'd in brutish sense.

*Momus.*—I concur; and am grown so weary of these tedious pleadings, as I'll pack up too and be gone. Besides, I see a crowd of other suitors pressing hither; I'll stop 'em, take their petitions, and prefer 'em above; and as I came in bluntly, without knocking, and nobody bid me welcome, so I'll depart as abruptly, without taking leave, and bid nobody farewell.

*Mercury.*—These, with forced reasons and strain'd
    arguments,
Urge vain pretences, whilst your actions plead,
And with a silent importunity

Awake the drowsy justice of the gods,
To crown your deeds with immortality.
The growing titles of your ancestors,
These nations' glorious acts, join'd to the stock
Of your own royal virtues, and the clear
Reflex they take from th' imitation
Of your famed court, make honour's story full,
And have to that secure fix'd state advanced
Both you and them, to which the labouring world,
Wading through streams of blood, sweats to aspire.
Those ancient worthies of these famous isles,
That long have slept, in fresh and lively shapes
Shall straight appear, where you shall see yourself
Circled with modern heroes, who shall be
In act, whatever elder times can boast,
Noble or great, as they in prophecy
Were all but what you are. Then shall you see
The sacred hand of bright Eternity
Mould you to stars, and fix you in the sphere.
To you, your royal half, to them she'll join
Such of this train, as with industrious steps
In the fair prints your virtuous feet have made,
Though with unequal paces, follow you.
This is decreed by Jove, which my return
Shall see perform'd; but first behold the rude
And old abiders here, and in them view
The point from which your full perfections grew.
You naked, ancient, wild inhabitants,
That breathed this air and press'd this flowery earth,
Come from those shades where dwells eternal night,
And see what wonders Time hath brought to light!

Atlas and the sphere vanisheth, and a new scene
appears, of mountains, whose eminent height
exceed the clouds, which past beneath them;
the lower parts were wild and woody: out of this
place comes forth a more grave Antimasque of
Picts, the natural inhabitants of this isle,
ancient Scots and Irish : these dance a Pyrrhica,
or martial dance.

When this Antimasque was past, there began to arise
out of the earth the top of a hill, which, by
little and little, grew to be a huge mountain,
that covered all the scene; the under-part of
this was wild and craggy, and above somewhat
more pleasant and flourishing; about the middle
part of this mountain were seated the three
kingdoms of England, Scotland, and Ireland, all
richly attired in regal habits, appropriated to the
several nations, with crowns on their heads, and
each of them bearing the ancient arms of the
kingdoms they represented. At a distance
above these, sat a young man in a white
embroidered robe ; upon his fair hair an olive
garland, with wings at his shoulders, and holding in his hand a cornucopia filled with corn
and fruits, representing the Genius of these
kingdoms.

l. 7. The 1634 and other editions have *Perica* for *Pyrrhica*.

### THE FIRST SONG.

*Genius.*

 Raise from these rocky cliffs your heads,
 Brave sons, and see where Glory spreads
 Her glittering wings; where Majesty,
 Crown'd with sweet smiles, shoots from her eye
 Diffusive joy! where Good and Fair
 United sit in Honour's chair.
Call forth your aged priests, and crystal streams,
To warm their hearts and waves in these bright beams!

*Kingdoms.*

1. From your consecrated woods,
 Holy Druids; 2. Silver floods,
 From your channels fringed with flowers,
3. Hither move; forsake your bowers,
1. Strew'd with hallowed oaken leaves,
 Deck'd with flags and sedgy sheaves,
2. And behold a wonder. 3. Say,
 What do your duller eyes survey?

*Chorus of Druids and Rivers.*

We see at once in dead of night,
A sun appear, and yet a bright
Noon-day springing from star-light.

*Genius.*

Look up, and see the darkened sphere
Deprived of light! her eyes shine there.

*Chorus.*

These are more sparkling than those were.

*Kingdoms.*

1. These shed a nobler influence;
2. These by a pure intelligence
    Of more transcendent virtue move;
3. These first feel, then kindle love;

1, 2. From the bosoms they inspire,
    These receive a mutual fire:
1, 2, 3. And where their flames impure return,
    These can quench, as well as burn.

*Genius.*

Here the fair victorious eyes
Make worth only Beauty's prize;
Here the hand of Virtue ties
'Bout the heart Love's amorous chain:
Captives triumph, vassals reign,
And none live here but the slain.

*Chorus.*

These are th' Hesperian bowers, whose fair trees bear
Rich golden fruit, and yet no dragon near.

*Genius.*

Then from your impris'ning womb,
Which is the cradle and the tomb

Of British worthies, fair sons, send
A troop of heroes, that may lend
Their hands to ease this laden grove,
And gather the ripe fruits of Love.

*Kingdoms.*

1, 2, 3. Open thy stony entrails wide,
And break, old Atlas, that the pride
Of three famed kingdoms may be spied.

*Chorus.*

Pace forth, thou mighty British Hercules,
With thy choice band, for only thou and these
May revel here in Love's Hesperides.

At this, the under-part of the rock opens, and out of a cave are seen to come the masquers, richly attired like ancient heroes, the colours yellow, embroidered with silver, their antique helms curiously wrought, and great plumes on the top; before them a troop of young lords and noblemen's sons, bearing torches of virgin-wax; these were apparelled after the old British fashion in white coats, embroidered with silver, girt and full gathered, cut square-collared, and round caps on their heads, with a white feather wreathen about them. First these dance with their lights in their hands, after which the masquers descend into the room, and dance their entry.

The dance being past, there appears in the further part of the heaven coming down a pleasant cloud, bright and transparent; which, coming softly downwards before the upper part of the mountain, embraceth the Genius, but so as through it all his body is seen; and then rising again with a gentle motion, bears up the Genius of the three kingdoms, and being past the airy region, pierceth the heavens, and is no more seen; at that instant, the rock with the three kingdoms on it sinks, and is hidden in the earth. This strange spectacle gave great cause of admiration, but especially how so huge a machine, and of that great height, could come from under the stage, which was but six foot high.

### THE SECOND SONG.

*Kingdoms.*

1. Here are shapes form'd fit for heaven;
2. Those move gracefully and even.
3. Here the air and paces meet,
   So just, as if the skilful feet
   Had struck the viols.—1, 2, 3. So the ear
   Might the tuneful footing hear.

*Chorus.*

And had the music silent been,
The eye a moving tune had seen.

*Genius.*

These must in the unpeopled sky
Succeed, and govern destiny :
Jove is tempering purer fire,
And will with brighter flames attire
These glorious lights.  I must ascend,
And help the work.

*Kingdoms.*

1. We cannot lend
Heaven so much treasure.  2. Nor that pay,
But rend'ring what it takes away.
3. Why should they, that here can move
So well, be ever fix'd above?

*Chorus.*

Or be to one eternal posture tied,
That can into such various figures slide?

*Genius.*

Jove shall not, to enrich the sky,
Beggar the earth : their fame shall fly
From hence alone, and in the sphere
Kindle new stars, whilst they rest here.

*Kingdoms.*

1, 2, 3. How can the shaft stay in the quiver,
Yet hit the mark?

*Genius.*
   Did not the river
  Eridanus the grace acquire
   In heaven and earth to flow:
  Above, in streams of golden fire,
   In silver waves below?

*Kingdoms.*
1, 2, 3. But shall not we, now thou art gone
   Who wert our Nature, wither,
  Or break that triple union
   Which thy soul held together?

*Genius.*
  In concord's pure immortal spring
   I will my force renew,
  And a more active virtue bring
   At my return. Adieu.

*Kingdoms.* Adieu.—*Chorus.* Adieu.

The Masquers dance their main dance; which done, the scene again is varied into a new and pleasant prospect, clean differing from all the other; the nearest part showing a delicious garden, with several walks and parterres set round with low trees, and on the sides, against these walks, were fountains and grots, and in the furthest part a palace, from whence went high walks upon arches, and above them open terraces planted with cypress trees; and all this together was composed of such ornaments as might express a princely villa.

From hence the Chorus, descending into the room, goes up to the State.

### THE THIRD SONG.

*By the Chorus going up to the Queen.*

Whilst thus the darlings of the gods
   From Honour's temple, to the shrine
Of Beauty, and these sweet abodes
   Of Love, we guide, let thy divine
Aspects, bright Deity! with fair
And halcyon beams becalm the air.

We bring Prince Arthur, or the brave
   St. George himself, great Queen, to you:
You'll soon discern him; and we have
   A Guy, a Bevis, or some true
Round-Table knight, as ever fought
For lady, to each beauty brought.

Plant in their martial hands, war's seat,
   Your peaceful pledges of warm snow,
And, if a speaking touch, repeat
   In Love's known language tales of woe,
Say, in soft whispers of the palm,
As eyes shoot darts, so lips shed balm.

For though you seem, like captives, led
   In triumph by the foe away,
Yet on the conqueror's neck you tread,
   And the fierce victor proves your prey;
What heart is then secure from you,
That can, though vanquish'd, yet subdue?

The song done, they retire, and the masquers dance the revels with the ladies, which continued a great part of the night.

The revels being past, and the King's Majesty seated under the State by the Queen, for conclusion to this masque there appears coming forth from one of the sides, as moving by a gentle wind, a great cloud, which, arriving at the middle of the heaven, stayeth; this was of several colours, and so great, that it covered the whole scene. Out of the further part of the heaven, begins to break forth two other clouds, differing in colour and shape; and being fully discovered, there appeared sitting in one of them Religion, Truth, and Wisdom. Religion was apparelled in white, and part of her face was covered with a light veil, in one hand a book, and in the other a flame of fire: Truth in a watchet robe, a sun upon her fore-head, and bearing in her hand a palm; Wisdom in a mantle wrought with eyes and hands, golden rays about her head, and Apollo's cithara in her hand. In the other cloud sate Concord, Government, and Reputation. The habit of Concord was carnation, bearing in her hand a little faggot of sticks bound together, and on the top of it a heart, and a garland of corn on her head. Government was figured in a coat of armour, bearing a shield, and on it a Medusa's head; upon her head a plumed helm, and in her right hand a lance. Reputation, a young man in purple robe wrought with gold, and wearing a laurel wreath on his head. These being come down in an equal distance to the middle part of the air, the great cloud began to break open, out of which struck beams of light; in the midst, suspended in the air, sat Eternity on a globe; his garment was long, of a light blue, wrought all over with stars of gold, and bearing in his hand a serpent bent into a circle, with his tail in his mouth. In the firmament about him was a troop of fifteen stars, expressing the stellifying of our British heroes; but one more great and eminent than the rest, which was over his head, figured his Majesty. And in the lower part was seen, afar off, the prospect of Windsor Castle, the famous seat of the most honourable Order of the Garter.

### THE FOURTH SONG.

*Eternity, Eusebeia, Aletheia, Sophia, Homonoia, Dicæarche, Euphemia.*

*Eternity.*

Be fixed, you rapid orbs, that bear
The changing seasons of the year
On your swift wings, and see the old
Decrepit sphere grown dark and cold;
Nor did Jove quench her fires: these bright
Flames have eclipsed her sullen light,

This Royal Pair, for whom Fate will
Make motion cease, and time stand still:
Since good is here so perfect, as no worth
Is left for after-ages to bring forth.

*Eusebeia.*

Mortality cannot with more
Religious zeal the Gods adore.

*Aletheia.*

My truths, from human eyes conceal'd,
Are naked to their sight reveal'd.

*Sophia.*

Nor do their actions from the guide
Of my exactest precepts slide.

*Homonoia.*

And as their own pure souls entwined,
So are their subjects' hearts combined.

*Dicæarche.*

So just, so gentle is their sway,
As it seems empire to obey.

*Euphemia.*

And their fair fame, like incense hurl'd
On altars, hath perfumed the world.

*Soph.* Wisdom.    *Aleth.* Truth.    *Euse.* Pure Adoration.
*Hom.* Concord.    *Dicæ.* Rule.    *Euphem.* Clear Reputation.

*Chorus.*

Crown this King, this Queen, this Nation!

*Chorus.*

Wisdom, truth, &c.

*Eternity.*

Brave spirits, whose advent'rous feet
  Have to the mountain's top aspired,
Where fair desert and honour meet,
  Here from the toiling press retired,
Secure from all disturbing evil,
For ever in my temple revel.

With wreaths of stars circled about,
  Gild all the spacious firmament,
And, smiling on the panting routs
  That labour in the steep ascent,
With your resistless influence guide
Of human change th' incertain tide.

*Eusebeia, Aletheia, Sophia.*

But oh, you Royal Turtles, shed,
  When you from earth remove,
On the ripe fruit of your chaste bed
  Those sacred seeds of love.

*Chorus.*

Which no power can but yours dispense,
Since you the pattern bear from hence.

*Homonoia, Dicæarche, Euphemia.*

Then from your fruitful race shall flow
　Endless succession :
Sceptres shall bud, and laurels blow
　'Bout their immortal throne.

*Chorus.*

Propitious stars shall crown each birth,
Whilst you rule them, and they the earth.

The song ended, the two clouds, with the persons sitting on them, ascend ; the great cloud closeth again, and so passeth away overthwart the scene, leaving behind it nothing but a serene sky. After which, the masquers dance their last dance, and the curtain was let fall.

## The Names of the Masquers.

### The King's Majesty.

Duke of Lennox,
Earl of Devonshire,
Earl of Holland,
Earl of Newport,
Earl of Elgin,
Viscount Grandison,
Lord Rich,
Lord Feilding,
Lord Digby,
Lord Dungarvan,
Lord Dunluce,
Lord Wharton,
Lord Paget,
Lord Salton.

### The Names of the young Lords and Noblemen's Sons.

Lord Walden,
Lord Cranborne,
Lord Brackley,
Lord Chandos,
Mr. William Herbert,
Mr. Thomas Howard,
Mr. Thomas Egerton,
Mr. Charles Cavendish,
Mr. Robert Howard,
Mr. Henry Spencer.

The Songs and Dialogues of this Book were set with apt Tunes to them, by Henry Lawes, one of His Majesty's Musicians.[1]

[1] This note first appeared in 1640 edition.

FINIS.

# NOTES

### p. 1. THE SPRING.

Much of this poem is modelled on some lines in Ronsard's *Amours de Marie.* Cf. especially ll. 13—16, and 20 to end, with

> "Icy, la bergerette en tournant son fuseau
> Desgoise ses amours, et là le pastoreau
> Respond à sa chanson : ici toute chose aime,
> Tout parle de l'amour, tout s'en veut enflammer.
> Seulement votre cœur, froid d'une glace extrême
> Demeure opiniastre et ne veut point aimer."

l. 3. *Candies the grass.* Fry justly compared the lines from Drayton's *Quest of Cynthia*—

> "Since when those frosts that winter brings,
>  Which candy every green."

### p. 2. TO A. L.

This lady remains unidentified. The suggestion that the initials stand for Anne Lovelace is highly improbable, as that lady married at the age of fifteen, and could hardly have stood in need of "persuasions to love."

### p. 5. LIPS AND EYES.

l. 7. Cf. Browne, *Britannia's Pastorals,* book ii. song 2, l. 214.

> "The fair Nereides,
> They came on shore and slily, as they fell,
> Convey'd each tear into an oyster-shell,
> And by some power that did affect the girls,
> Transform'd those liquid drops to orient pearls."

p. 7. A BEAUTIFUL MISTRESS.

This song was set to music, and republished in Lawes' *Ayres and Dialogues*, 1653.

p. 10. MY MISTRESS COMMANDING ME TO RETURN HER LETTERS.

l. 78. *trifling hearts.* Cf. Donne, *The Broken Heart*, l. 9.
"Ah, what a trifle is a heart."

p. 13. SECRECY PROTESTED.

ll. 11 to end. Cf. Donne, *The Damp.*

"When I am dead, and doctors know not why,
And my friends' curiosity
Will have me cut up to survey each part,
When they shall find your picture in my heart. . . ."

This poem was included in the 1655 edition of Lawes' *Ayres and Dialogues.*

p. 16. MEDIOCRITY IN LOVE REJECTED.

It has been thought that the idea of this poem may have been suggested by the French lines beginning,

"Donne moi plus de pitié ou plus de creaulté,"

which were translated by Lovelace.

p. 17. GOOD COUNSEL.

l. 15. *Calenture,* a burning fever. Cf. p. 43, l. 42.

p. 18. AN EDDY.

This and the succeeding poem were printed in the volume of Pembroke and Rudyard's Poems, 1660, to many of which the alleged authors had no sort of claim.

The "conceit" would seem to have been suggested to Carew by the following lines in Donne's Elegy vi.—

"When I behold a stream, which from the spring
Doth with doubtful melodious murmuring,
Or in a speechless slumber, calmly ride
Her wedded channel's bosom, and there chide,
And bend her brows, and swell, if any bough
Do but stoop down to kiss her utmost brow;

# NOTES. 239

> Yet, if her gnawing kisses win
> The traitorous banks to gape, and let her in,
> She rusheth violently, and doth divorce
> Her from her native and her long-kept course,
> And roars and braves it, and in gallant scorn,
> In flattering eddies promising return,
> She flouts her channel, which thenceforth is dry;
> Then say I; 'That is she, and this am I.' "

### p. 19. CONQUEST BY FLIGHT.

The second portion of this song, commencing "Young men fly," was adopted by Samuel Pick for his volumes of selections purporting to be his own composition, *Festum Voluptatis*, 1639.

### p. 20. TO MY INCONSTANT MISTRESS.

The first and third stanzas of this poem were set to music by Lawes (*Ayres and Dialogues*, 1653, p. 8).

### p. 23. INGRATEFUL BEAUTY THREATENED.

Antony à Wood mentions a translation into Latin elegiac verse of these lines by Henry Jacob, of Merton College, Oxford (Carew's college), who was in his opinion, "the greatest prodigy of criticism in his time." Jacob's verson has been preserved in *Philologiae* Ἀνακαλυπτήριον, *Oratione celebratum Inaugurali quam publice habuit ad Oxonio-Mertonenses Henricus Jacobius. Publicavit à quindecennio H. B. à Coll. Oxon. Omn. Animar.* 1652. On page 47 appears *Interpretatio* ἀντίτεχνος *ex Anglico Thomas Carew: Ad ingrate Pulchram*, as follows—

> "Ne levis ignores: quae sit laudata superbis
>   (Coelia) sum laudis conditor ipse tuae.
> Inter inauspicuum formâ tu congrege vulgum
>   Respisses, paritas quas inhonora gravat:
> Vexerat eximium Noster nisi nomen Apollo
>   Praepetior Famae quo movet ala tuae.
> Sirenem loqueris? cernis Basiliscon? at illa
>   Arma ministrantem me fateare reum.
> Dulce tuum amare mei fit mumeris, omne venustum:
>   Nostra micas nostro stella locata polo.
> Fulgure quid tantum saevire praecarius aether
>   (Indiges authori tu male grata!) velit?
> Parce movere minis. Laesus ne infecta refingam,
>   Quae feci pollens. Parce movere minis.
> Mystica percellant hebetem proscenia formae;
>   Tu mihi mortali flore caduca pates.
> Quod figmentosê velarunt cortice Vates,
>   Pelluxit veri singula larva catis."

**l. 6.** *imp'd*, a term borrowed from the language of falconry signifying, to graft a new feather on a wing: cf. the German verb *impfen*. The word was a favourite one with the poets, and was used, as by Carew, metaphorically, by Spenser, Shakespeare, Fletcher, Massinger, Milton and others.

### p. 24. DISDAIN RETURNED.

The first two stanzas of this well-known poem were printed, set to music, in Porter's *Madrigals and Airs*, 1632, and again in Lawes' *Ayres and Dialogues*, 1653.

### p. 25. A LOOKING-GLASS.

Another version of this poem, consisting of the two first stanzas as in the text, and five others, quite different, occurs in MS. Harl. 6057, f. 8.

> "This flattering glass, whose smooth face wears
> Your shadow, which a sun appears,
> Was once a river of my tears,
>
> About your cold heart they did make
> A circle, where the briny lake
> Congeal'd into a crystal cake.
>
> This glass and shadow seem to say,
> 'Like us, the beauties you survey
> Will quickly break, or fly away.'
>
> Since then my tears can only show
> You your own face, you cannot know
> How fair you are, but by my woe.
>
> Nor had the world else known your name,
> But that my sad verse spread the fame
> Of thee, most fair and cruel dame!
>
> Forsake but your disdainful mind,
> And in my songs the world shall find
> That you are not more fair than kind.
>
> Change but your scorn: my verse shall chase
> Decay far from you, and your face
> Shall shine with an immortal grace.

### p. 26. AN ELEGY ON THE LA. PEN.

This lady was Martha, the fourth of the nine daughters of Sir Thomas Temple by his wife Esther (daughter of Miles Sandys of Latimers, Bucks), who is said to have lived to see seven hundred descendants of her body. Martha married Sir Thomas Peniston of Leigh, Sussex, and died January 4, 1620. The elegy was, therefore, composed while Carew was attending Lord Herbert of Cherbury, in Paris.

## NOTES.

l. 74. *blubber'd eyes.* A too favourite expression of Carew's; cf. pp. 111, l. 16, 113, l. 15.

### p. 29. TO MY MISTRESS IN ABSENCE.

Cf. Donne's *Valediction forbidding Mourning.* (Muses' Library Edition, i. 51.)

### p. 30. TO HER IN ABSENCE.

l. 14. Cf. Aurelian Townsend's lines—

"Those arms wherein wide open
Love's fleet was wont to put."

### p. 31. ETERNITY OF LOVE PROTESTED.

ll. 9—16. Cf. the eleventh stanza of Donne's *Eclogue at the Marriage of the Earl of Somerset* (Muses' Library Edition, i. 97)—

"Now, as in Tullia's tomb, one lamp burnt clear," κ.τ.λ.

### p. 35. TO T. H.

The identity of this "fair copy" of Celia is as unknown as that of the original.

ll. 16, 17. Cf. Donne's *Dream.*

"Image of her whom I love, more than she,
Whose fair impression in my faithful heart
Makes me her medal, and makes her love me,
As kings do coins, to which their stamp impart
The value."

### p. 36. TO SAXHAM.

Saxham Parva was the seat of Sir John Crofts, whose third son John was one of Carew's companions in France. Sir John died in 1628, aged sixty-six. By his wife Maria, daughter of Thomas Shirley, he had issue three sons, Henry, Anthony, and John; and eight daughters, Anna (m. Thomas Lord Wentworth), Francisca (m. (1) John Crompton, (2) Edmund Poley), Jana (m. Humphrey Mildmay), Dorothea (m. Sir John Bennett), Alice (m. Sir Owen Smith), Arabella (m. Sir W. Bryers), Cecilia (m. Thomas Killigrew), and Maria (m. Christopher Abdy). Carew appears to have stayed with the family at Saxham, more than once. Internal evidence makes it appear probable that before composing this address to Saxham, Carew had somewhat carefully studied Ben Jonson's address to Penshurst.

l. 18. *volary*=aviary.

### p. 39. UPON A RIBBON.

l. 1. *This silken wreath, which circles in mine arm.* Cf. Donne's *Funeral* (Muses' Library Edition, i. 61)—

"That subtle wreath of hair which **crowns my arm.**"

This, though the closest, is not the only resemblance between the two poems.

### p. 40. TO THE KING.

King James I. was fond of visiting Saxham on his Progresses. Chamberlain wrote to Carleton 12 Feb. 16 $\frac{18}{19}$: "I hear the King will be here within the fortnight. They pass the time merrily at Newmarket. Lately they have been at Sir John Crofts', near Bury, and in requital those ladies have invited them to a **masque** of their own invention, all those fair sisters (see note to p. 36, above) being summoned for the purpose, so that on Thursday next the King, Prince, and all the Court go thither a-shroving." And again 16 Feb. **16** $\frac{21}{22}$: "The King is still at Newmarket. He is to go next week a-shroving to Sir John Crofts'. That Lady and her daughter Cecily have been much at Newmarket of late."

The heading of this **address to the King** denotes that it was written by Carew for some such occasion, to be spoken by his friend John Crofts.

Charles I. was often a visitor to Newmarket, and may also have visited Saxham, but it is more likely that this welcome was to his **father.**

### p. 42. UPON THE SICKNESS OF E. S.

The identity of E. S. is equally mysterious as most of the other ladies addressed in verse by Carew.

l. 36. Cf. Donne, *To his Mistress Going to Bed* (Muses' Library Edition, i. 148)—

"Off with your wiry coronet, and show
The hairy diadems which on you do grow."

### p. 44. TO LUCINDA.

This lady was **Lucy** Percy, daughter of Henry, Earl of Northumberland, and second wife of James Hay, first Earl of Carlisle, whom she married Nov. 6, 1617. She was famous as a "busy stateswoman," no less than for her wit and beauty, and is said to have numbered both the Earl of Strafford and Pym among her active lovers. Herrick and Waller, among others, decorously celebrated her charms, and broad hints of her more secret attractions were given by Suckling, in his verses *Upon my Lady Carlisle's walking in Hampton Court*

*Gardens*, a poem in the form of a dialogue between T. C. and J. S. It is generally assumed that the "T. C." of the dialogue is Carew, and, if so, Carew had a more intimate knowledge of Lucinda's beauties than Suckling himself, who elsewhere professed that a look from the lady's eyes only was sufficient to account for his death.

The lady became a widow in 1636, and died 1660, aged sixty-one.

In a private MS. to which Mr. Hazlitt had access, the date of this poem is given as 1632.

### p. 48. UPON THE KING'S SICKNESS.

Commentators have agreed in assigning as the occasion of this courtier's address the attack of small-pox from which Charles I. suffered in 1633. But lines 29—40 apparently refer to the king's son, and even a laureate would scarcely write of the "dread command" of a child, aged three, and would hesitate to attribute to him so much sympathy as is implied in a clouded brow and tearful eyes. It would seem more probable, therefore, that the invalid was James I.

### p. 50. TO A LADY NOT YET ENJOYED.

l. 3. *Shall a pure wreath of eye-beams twine.* Cf. Donne's *Ecstasy*, l. 7—

"Our eye-beams twisted, and did thread
Our eyes upon one double string."

### p. 52. A FLY THAT FLEW.

R. Fletcher, who was a friend of Carew, has in his *Ex otio Negotium* (1656) some lines with a similar title, amongst them the following, which seem to have suggested, or been suggested by, ll. 14—16 of Carew's poem,

"Or didst thou think to rival all
Don Phaethon and his great fall?
And in a richer sea of brine
Drown Icarus again in thine?"

The same verses appear in most editions of Cleveland's poems.

### p. 53. CELIA SINGING.

In several MS. copies of this song, its occasion is stated to have been the singing of "Celia to her lute in the vault at York House"; in others, "in Arundel Garden." The reputation of the Arundel marbles has led most editors to declare the latter ascription to be correct.

## NOTES.

**p. 56. IN THE PERSON OF A LADY.**

Set to music in Lawes' *Ayres and Dialogues*, 1653, p. 9.

**p. 60. A PASTORAL DIALOGUE.**

Set to music in Lawes' *Ayres and Dialogues*, 1653, p. 5.

**p. 64. A PASTORAL DIALOGUE.**

ll. 6—16. It is easy to believe that the Shepherd and Nymph had witnessed a performance of *Romeo and Juliet*, and retained a lively memory of the language used by Shakspere's lovers at their parting after the night spent together. Cf. **act iii. sc. 5.**

**p. 67. TO MY COUSIN (C. R.) MARRYING MY LADY (A).**

Probably C. R. stands for Carew Ralegh, the second son of Sir Walter, who married Philippa, the rich widow of Sir Antony Ashley (Lady A.). Carew Ralegh was, like Carew, a gentleman of the privy chamber, and he owned a seat at Horsley, where Carew stayed with him. The cousinship claimed in the title is not to be pressed too far. Carew Ralegh's mother was the sister of Sir Nicholas Throckmorton, who was the adopted heir of his uncle Sir Francis Carew, **and** who assumed the name and arms of Carew. But **the connexion** between the **two** families of Carew **was of the** slightest.

**p. 68. A LOVER CONSULTS WITH REASON.**

Set to music in Lawes' *Ayres and Dialogues*, 1655, p. 30.

**p. 70. A RAPTURE.**

The freedom of expression exhibited by Carew in this, his longest poem, appears to have been a subject of reproach to the writer among some of his well-wishing friends. Carew was made to tender a tardy apology for his bold verse in *The great Assizes holden in Parnassus by Apollo and his Assessors*: 1640, a skit attributed to the pen of George Wither. The subject-matter of the "Assizes" was the licence of the many news-sheets of the time, which were severally summoned and put on trial before a court consisting of Apollo, Lord Verulam, Sir Philip Sidney, Julius Cæsar, Scaliger, Erasmus, and others, and a jury which included Wither, Carew, May, Davenant, Drayton, Beaumont, Fletcher, Heywood, Shakspere, Massinger, Sylvester, and Sandys; John Taylor being Court-crier, Ben Jonson Keeper of the Trophonian Den, and Edmund Spenser Clerk of the Assizes. When it came to the turn of Writer of Occurrences to be tried, he replied to the charge with a "flat negative"—

# NOTES. 245

"The pris'ner also craved he might be heard
While he against a juryman preferred
A just exception: his request was granted,
And, fraught with malice, though much wit he wanted,
He gentle Mr. Cary did refuse,
Who pleased the ladies with his courtly muse:
He said that he, by his luxurious pen,
Deserved had better the Trophonian Den
Than many now which stood to be arraigned;
For he the Thespian fountain had distained
With foul conceits, and made their waters bright
Impure, like those of the Hermaphrodite.
He said that he in verse more loose had been
Than old Chærephanes or Aretine
In obscene portraitures, and that his fellow
In Helicon had reared the first Burdello;
That he had changed the chaste Castalian spring
Into a Carian well, whose waters bring
Effeminate desires and thoughts unclean
To minds that erst were pure and most serene.
Thus spake the pris'ner when a furious glance
Was darted from Apollo's countenance,
Which struck him dumb: then Scaliger, the wise
Was call'd, to whom Apollo thus applies
His speech."

Apollo expresses his opinion that Scaliger, the censor of manners in Parnassus, would not permit such crimes as have been ascribed to Carew; Scaliger replies—

"I have, my Sovereign dear
With care intended what concerns my place,
So to conserve your springs from mixtures base;
Yet all my care and labour is but vain
Except Jove will consent t' undo again
His work of human nature, and the same
Of such pure stuff and perfect temper frame
As it of no corruption may admit:
For I have tried my industry and wit
Both art and authors to refine and mend,
As well as times, yet can I not defend
But some luxuriant wit will often vent
Lascivious poems against my consent:
Of which offence if Cary guilty be,
Yet may some chaster songs him render free
From censure sharp, and expiate those crimes
Which are not fully his, but rather Time's:
But let your grace vouchsafe that he may try
How he can make his own apology."

> Apollo here gave Cary leave to speak—
> Who thus in modest sort did silence break.
>
> "In wisdom's nonage and unriper years
> Some lines slipp'd from my pen, which since with tears
> I labour'd to expunge. This song of mine
> Was not infusèd by the Virgins nine,
> Nor through my dreams divine upon this hill
> Did this vain *Rapture* issue from my quill.
> No Thespian waters but a Paphian fire
> Did me with this foul ecstasy inspire:
> I oft have wish'd that I (like Saturn) might
> This infant of my folly smother quite,
> Or that I could retract what I had done
> Into the bosom of oblivion."
>
> Thus Cary did conclude, for press'd **by grief**
> He was compell'd to be concise **and brief.**
> Phœbus at his contrition did **relent,**
> And edicts soon through all Parnassus **sent,**
> That none should dare to attribute the shame
> Of that fond *Rapture* unto Cary's name,
> But ordered that the infamy should light
> On those who did the same read or **recite.**

Another allusion to **the** poem is in *Stipendiariae* **Lachrymae** (1654), where the **author** describes a visit to the shades—

> "There, purged of the folly of disdaining,
> Laura walk'd hand in hand with Petrarch join'd,
> No more of Tyrant Goblin Honour plaining:
> There Sidney in rich Stella's arms lay twined;
> Carew and Suckling there mine eyes did find."

Donne may possibly have furnished Carew with the text of his *Rapture;* cf. *The Damp* (Muses' Library Edition, i. p. 68)—

> "If you dare be brave,
> And pleasure in your conquest have,
> First kill the enormous giant, your Disdain;
> And let th' enchantress Honour, next be slain."

In more than one passage the poem is closely modelled on the speech of Petronius in *The Tragedy of Nero,* act iv. sc. 7.

ll. 3—10. Carew has invested Honour with the attributes of the porter in Donne's Elegy *The Perfume,* and in styling him a "Swiss" gives him the name of a footman. Cf. ll. 31—34,

> "The grim eight-foot-high iron-bound serving-man,
> \*    \*    \*    \*    \*
> He that, to bar the first gate, doth as wide
> As the great Rhodian Colossus stride."

l. 27. *ivy-twines.* Cf. Donne, Elegy viii. l. 59—

"Let our arms clasp like ivy."

l. 74. *mintage, coins.* Donne has the like image; cf. *A Valediction of Weeping*, ll. 3, 4—

"Thy face coins them . . .
And by this mintage they are something worth."

l. 76. Cf. Donne, Elegy ix. ll. 35—8—

"Then like the chemic's masculine equal fire,
Which in the limbec's warm womb doth inspire
Into th' earth's worthless dirt a soul of gold."

l. 103. *Nor are we betrayed,* etc. Cf. Donne's *Valediction of my Name,* ll. 49, 50—

"And when thy melted maid
Corrupted by thy lover's gold."

l. 116. *Aretine.* Pietro Aretine, born at Arezzo (whence he derived his name) in 1492, was the father of literary blackmailing. He sprang into unenviable fame as the author of sixteen sonnets which he composed for some naturalistic drawings designed by Julio Romano, and engraved by Marc Antonio Raimondi. He died 1556.

l. 145, 146. *Love's exchequer.* Cf. Donne, Elegy xix. ll. 91—94—

"Rich Nature in women wisely made
Two purses, and their mouths aversely laid.
They then, which to the lower tribute owe,
That way which that exchequer looks must go."

ll. 151—3. Cf. Donne's Elegy iii. ll. 12—14—

"Shall women, more hot, wily, wild than these,
Be bound to one man, and did nature then
Idly make them apter to endure than men?"

Cleveland has a poem entitled, *To Chloris: A Rapture,* beginning, "Come, Julia, come."

### p. 76. EPITAPH ON THE LADY MARY VILLIERS.

There seems to be no record of a Lady Mary Villiers who died in infancy. Carew has elegies on the Duke of Buckingham and his brother, Christopher, the Earl of Anglesey, with both of whom he seems to have been acquainted, but Mary Villiers, the daughter of the Duke, was three times married, and lived to see James II. on the throne.

## p. 76. ANOTHER.

ll. 1—4. The idea is repeated by Carew in his Epitaph on Maria Wentworth. Cf. p. 79, ll. 1—3.

## p. 78. EPITAPH ON THE LADY S.

This lady was almost certainly Mary, wife of Sir William Salter, one of the King's Carvers-in-ordinary, and daughter of Sir Thomas Sherland of Wilshall, Suffolk. She died April 24, 1631, aged 30, and was buried in the church of Iver, Bucks.

## p. 79. MARIA WENTWORTH.

These verses were written as an inscription for the tomb of Mary Wentworth, second daughter of Thomas, Earl of Cleveland, by Anna, daughter of Sir John Crofts, and sister of Carew's friend John Crofts. She died in 1632, aged 18, and the sum of £2000 is said to have been expended on her monument in the church of Toddington, Beds. Carew's lines, or rather the first six stanzas, were duly cut in the stone, and have often been cited in collections of quaint epitaphs. Something seems wrong in the Latinity of the heading.

ll. 5, 6. Cf. Donne, *Anatomy of the World*, ll. 83, 4—

"This to thy soul allow,
Think thy shell broke, think thy soul hatch'd but now."

l. 15. Cf. Donne, *ib.* l. 368—

"Only herself except, she pardon'd all."

## p. 80. ON THE DUKE OF BUCKINGHAM.

The favourite of James I., assassinated by Felton, Aug. 23, 1628.

## p. 83. FOUR SONGS.

It has not been found possible to identify the play, if it has come down to us, for which these songs were written "by way of chorus." Thomas Killigrew introduced the first song, *Of Jealousy*, into his play *Cicilia and Clorinda* (Part II. Act V. sc. ii.), written at Florence in 1651, and added the following note—

"This chorus was written by Mr. Thomas Carew, cupbearer to Charles I., and sung in a Masque at Whitehall 1633. And I presume to make use of it here, because in the first design, 'twas writ at my request upon a dispute held between Mistress Cecilia Crofts and myself, when he was present; she being then a maid-of-honour. This I have set down, lest any man should believe me so foolish as to steal such a poem from so famous an author; or so vain as to pretend to the making of it myself; and those that are not satisfied with this apology, and this song in this place, I am always ready to give them a worse of my own."

The songs seem to fit none of the plays or masques that are known to have been produced in 1633. Mr. Fleay (*Eng. Drama*, ii. 239) expresses the opinion that Shirley's *Arcadia* was the play for which the songs were written, as in it there is a lover disguised as an Amazon, but there is no lady rescued from death by a knight, who instantly leaves her, in the play, nor are the choruses appropriate.

Killigrew married Cecilia Crofts ; *v.* p. 111.

### p. 85. FEMININE HONOUR.

l. 4. *culters*, ploughshares. The allusion is to the ordeal by fire, which provided for the establishment of the innocence of a suspected person by his or her ablility to walk, blindfold and barefooted, over nine red-hot ploughshares.

### p. 87. INCOMMUNICABILITY OF LOVE.

This song is based upon Donne's *Confined Love* (Muses' Library Edition, i. 37).

ll. 8—12. Cf. Donne's *Letter to the Countess of Huntingdon*, ll. 125—128.

> "He much profanes whom valiant heats do move
> To style his wandering rage of passion, love ;
> Love that imparts in everything delight
> Is fancied in the soul, not in the sight."

### p. 90. TO BEN JONSON.

*The New Inn* was produced 19 Jan. 16 28/29 and was hissed from the stage, so that even the first performance was unfinished. In publishing the play Jonson, soured and infirm, annexed the Ode in which he exhorted himself to—

> "Come, leave the loathsome stage,
> And the more loathsome age."

The lines were parodied freely by his enemies, and the "sons of Ben" rallied round him with counter demonstrations, of which the present example was contributed by Carew.

l. 31. *Goodwin*, the quicksands on the Kentish coast.

### p. 94. TO THE LADY ANNE HAY.

Honora Denny, daughter of Sir Edward Denny, Earl of Norwich, married James, Lord Hay of Sawley (created Earl of Carlisle in 1622), and became the mother of Lady Anne Hay; hence the allusion in l. 16. Carew himself was through his grandmother, Martha Denny, distantly connected with Lady Carlisle: cf. also l. 71.

l. 7. If the sense is to be pressed, this line is a curious confession of callousness on the part of a poet who had lost both parents and other near relatives.

ll. 34, 35. Cf. Donne's *Letter to the Countess of Huntingdon*,

"You are the straight line."

### p. 97. TO THE COUNTESS OF ANGLESEY.

This lady was Elizabeth, daughter of Thomas Sheldon of Houby, Leicester. She married Christopher Villiers, the younger brother of the Duke of Buckingham, who was created Earl of Anglesey 1623, and died 1630.

l. 72. It would appear that there had been some opposition to the match of Christopher Villiers with Elizabeth Sheldon, and that Carew played the part of go-between to the distressed lovers.

### p. 100. ELEGY ON DR. DONNE.

Donne died March 31, 1631. Carew's elegy, which seems to express, as indeed it might, sincere admiration of its subject's genius and to have been inspired by genuine feeling, was first published in the first edition of Donne's poems, 1633.

l. 4. *dough-baked.* This ugly word is Donne's. Cf. his *Letter to the Lady Carey and Mistress Essex Rich, from Amiens,* l. 20—

"In dough-baked men some harmlessness we see."

l. 25. "*The Muses' garden, with pedantic weeds
O'erspread, was purged by thee : the lazy seeds
Of servile imitation thrown away.*"

Cf. Donne, *Letter to Mr.* **Rowland Woodward**—

". . . So affects my muse, now, a chaste fallowness,
Since she to few, yet to too many hath shown,
How love-song weeds and satiric thorns are grown
Where seeds of better arts were early sown."

### p. 104. IN ANSWER OF AN ELEGIACAL LETTER FROM AURELIAN TOWNSEND.

Too little is known of Townsend, described by Philip, Earl of Pembroke as "a poor and pocky poet, but a married man and a housekeeper in Barbican, hard by the now Earl of Bridgewater's. He hath a very fine and fair daughter, mistress to the Palsgrave first, and then afterwards [to] the noble Count

of Dorset, a Privy Councillor and a Knight of the Garter.
Aurelian would be glad to sell an 100 verses at sixpence a
piece, 50 shillings an 100 verses." In 1601 Townsend was
steward to Robert, Earl of Salisbury; in 1608, he accompanied
Lord Herbert of Cherbury, to France, and was said by him
to be a gentleman "that spoke the languages of French, Italian,
and Spanish in great perfection"; he married Anne, widow of
William Agborough, and before 1632 was father of five children;
in 1633 he, or another student of the same name, was entered
at Gray's Inn. His later years appear to have been troublous,
and if not actually imprisoned for debt, he came very near it.
His "fine and fair daughter," Mary, finally married George
Kirke in 1646, and was given away by the King, "she being
the admired beauty of the times;" she became the mother of
the celebrated Diana de Vere, the second wife of the twentieth
and last Earl of Oxford, and lived till 1701. Townsend is,
perhaps, best known as the author selected by Inigo Jones to
replace Jonson as writer of court masques. Two of these,
*Albion's Triumph* and *Tempe Restored*, both produced early in
1632, were printed.

In l. 54 Carew mentions the *Shepherd's Paradise* as being
the creation of Townsend, but the masque so named has always
been attributed to Walter Montague; yet it is a strange mis-
take for Carew, who knew both men well, to have made.
Townsend's "elegiacal letter" to Carew, if it exists, has yet to
be unearthed. There are several anonymous poems in the
miscellanies on the subject of Gustavus Adolphus' death, but
none appear to contain the invitation to Carew. Some of
Townsend's poems are of no ordinary merit, and the discovery
of more of them were very desirable.

Gustavus Adolphus was killed November 6, 1632.

l. 24. *Our romances of The Knight o' th' Sun.* The Knight
of the Sun was Alfebo, son of the Emperor Trebacio, and the
original story of his exploits is to be sought in *Espejo de Principes
y Caballeros*, by Diego Ortunez, 1562.

p. 108. UPON MASTER MONTAGUE.

"Wat" Montague, son of Henry Montague, Recorder and
M.P. for the City of London, and first Earl of Manchester,
was born in 1604. His life was eventful and varied. Employed
on secret service by Buckingham, he made several journeys to
France, till in 1627 he was imprisoned there. He returned to
England in 1633, which is probably the date of Carew's poetical
addresses to him, and in the same year his *Shepherd's
Paradise* was produced (*v.* p. 106 and note). On a visit to
Rome in 1639, he embraced the Romish faith, and, though
appointed Chamberlain to the Queen, was later imprisoned in

the Tower. Banished with Sir Kenelm **Digby** in 1649, he retired to Pontoise, where he became Abbot, **and died in** 1677.

*The Shepherd's Paradise; a comedy privately acted before the late King Charles by the Queen's Majesty and Ladies of Honour,* was first published in 1659, apparently without the knowledge or authority of Montague. The publisher declared in a preface that he knew for a fact that Montague was the author, rather implying that the question had been in doubt.

l. 22. *The halcyon sits, &c.* Cf. Browne, *Brit. Past.* ii. 1—

"**As smooth as** when the halcyon builds her nest."

### p. 111. THE MARRIAGE OF T. K. AND C. C.

T. K. was Thomas Killigrew, and C. C., Cecilia Crofts, a daughter of Sir John Crofts of Saxham, and a maid-of-honour to Queen Henrietta Maria. The marriage took place at Oatlands, June 29, 1636, and April 16, 1637, was baptized at St. Martins-in-the-Fields, Henry Killigrew, the only issue of the union, which was dissolved by the death of Cecilia, January 1 following. She was buried in Westminster Abbey.

### p. 115. UPON MY LORD CHIEF JUSTICE. HIS ELECTION OF MY LADY A. W.

The Lord Chief Justice was Sir **John** Finch, Baron Finch of Fordwich (b. 1584, d. 1660), who was appointed to his high judicial office October 16, 1634. The lady whom he "elected for his mistress" is always said to have been Lady Anne Wentworth, third daughter of the Earl of Cleveland. Finch must have shared Carew's taste for a "wench about thirteen," but Lady Anne escaped **him,** and on July 9, 1638, at the age of 15, married John Lord Lovelace, Baron of Hurley, Berks. Finch was twice married, first to Eleanor Wyatt, and secondly to Mabel Fotherby.

### p. 117. TO A. D.

Another unidentified Lady.

l. 21. *specular stone.* Cf. Donne, *The Undertaking*, l. 6, "the skill of specular stone;" and his *Letter to the Countess of Bedford*, l. 29, "the use of specular stone."

l. 35. Cf. p. 87, ll. 9—12.

### p. 120. TO MY FRIEND G. N.

It has been assumed that **the** initials G. N. must stand for Gilbert Neville, though no reason has ever been given. Wrest Park was the seat of the Grey family, but nothing is known of Carew's connexion with any member of it.

It is apparent from the opening and closing lines of this **verse**-letter that Carew had been engaged in some fighting expedition in the north of England. It is not impossible that this expedition was that organized and fitted **out at** great expense by Carew's friend, Sir John Suckling, **but no** other evidence to connect him with it has been found.

l. 23. *touch.* Basanites, the dark stone used for testing gold, and known formerly as *lapis Lydius*, was known as "touch."

In the "Funeral Elegy," in his *Anatomy of the World*, Donne has the line—

"Alas! what's marble, jet, or porphyry?"

Cf. also W. Drummond's *Epitaph*,

"Though marble, porphyry and burning touch
May praise these spoils, yet can they not too **much**."

### p. 124. A NEW YEAR'S GIFT TO THE KING.

It is a coincidence that Jonson also has *A New Year's Gift, sung to the King*, 1635," commencing (after a prelude) with the words, "*To-day old Janus opens the new year.*"

### p. 126. FOR THE COUNTESS OF CARLISLE.

For the Countess, *v.* p. 44 and note.

### p. 128. TO MY HONOURED FRIEND MASTER THOMAS MAY.

Carew's address to May was prefixed to the printed copy of *The Heir; a comedy as it was acted by the Company of the Revels*, 1620, first published in 1622. Thomas May (born 1595), though he wrote several plays, is better known as the translator of Virgil's *Georgics* and of Lucan's *Pharsalia*, and as the historian of the Long Parliament. His failure to get the appointment of City Chronologer is said to have accounted for his adhesion to the Parliamentary party. According to Wood, he was a debauchee, and kept "beastly and atheistical company." He died 1650.

### p. 129. TO MY WORTHY FRIEND MASTER GEORGE SANDYS.

George Sandys was born 1578, and was the seventh son of Edwin Sandys, Archbishop of York. He was largely interested in colonial enterprise, in Virginia and the Bermudas, and resided for some time in America, where he wrote part of his translation of Ovid's *Metamorphoses*, completed in 1629. His *Paraphrase upon the Psalms and upon the Hymns dispersed through the Old and New Testament* was first published in 1636, and reappeared in more gorgeous style with Carew's eulogistic verses in 1638. He died 1644.

p. 131. TO MY FRIEND HENRY, LORD CAREY OF LEPPINGTON.

**Henry,** Lord Carey of Leppington, **was** the eldest son of the **Earl of M**onmouth, whom he succeeded in title in 1639, and elder brother **of** Thomas Carey the poet, whose history has been so much confounded with that of Thomas Carew. The book to which Carew's lines were prefixed in company with productions from the pens of Davenant, Suckling, and Aurelian Townsend, was *Romulus and Tarquin: First written in Italian, and now taught English.* The first edition appeared in 1637, and was followed by others in 1638 and 1648. It was a rendering of *Il Romulo* and *Il Tarquinio Superbo*, by Vergilio, Marquis de Malvezzi (b. 1599, d. 1654), who once came as ambassador to England.

l. 8. *Bembo.* A cardinal and noted writer, who made it his aim to restore pure Latinity. He refused to read his Breviary in Latin lest it should **corrupt** his style. He was born **1470,** and died 1547.

l. 9. *Varchi.* A poet and historian, born 1502, died 1562.

l. 9. *The Crusca.* The celebrated literary Academy of Florence, which in 1612 first published its Dictionary of pure Italian.

p. 132. TO MY WORTHY FRIEND MASTER DAVENANT.

*The Just Italian,* originally **produced at the** Blackfriars Theatre, was published in 1630.

l. 24. *Red Bull and Cock-pit flight.* The Red Bull Theatre was situated at the top of St. John's Street, Clerkenwell, and the Cockpit in Drury Lane. If neither house had the prestige of the Blackfriars, many excellent plays were produced at each of them, and Davenant himself came to be governor **of the** King and Queen's Company acting at the Cockpit.

p. 133. TO THE READER OF MASTER WILLIAM DAVENANT'S PLAY.

The play referred to is *The Wits,* a comedy produced at the Blackfriars Theatre, January **28, 1634,** and published with these lines prefixed **in** 1636.

p. 135. TO MY FRIEND WILL. DAVENANT.

This address to Davenant was prefixed to the first edition of his *Madagascar, with other Poems,* 1638. In the 1640 and subsequent editions of Carew's poems the first fourteen lines were omitted, and replaced by Habington's contribution to the same volume, commencing, "I crowded 'mongst the **first** to see the stage." Habington's fourteen lines are complete in themselves, but they appeared among Carew's poems with the last six lines of Carew's address tacked on to them. Mr. Ebsworth was the first to point out this curious blunder of the compiler of Carew's works. No earlier editor had troubled to compare the lines as they appeared in the 1640 edition with the earlier version prefixed to *Madagascar*.

### p. 137. THE COMPLEMENT.

It would be difficult to name with confidence the first poet who explained in verse to his mistress for what he loved her not and for what he loved her. Carew was certainly not the first, and took no pains to conceal the fact. The last line of his *Complement* was taken almost literally from Marlowe's "I love thee not for sacred chastity," the concluding couplet of which runs,

"I love thee not for voice or slender small,
But wilt thou know wherefore, fair sweet, for all."

l. 16. *None can paint their white and red.* It has been suggested on MS. authority that the true reading is *None can part*, which gives, perhaps, a better sense, and support of a kind is lent to this view by the fact that Donne had anticipated the idea. Cf. *Anatomy of the World*, ll. 123—5,

"She, whose complexion was so even made
That which of her ingredients should invade
The other three, no fear, no art could guess."

### p. 141. A SONG.

This poem is remarkable for (besides its rare beauty) the number of imitations and parodies which it inspired. The collections of verse which were gathered from all quarters and published together after the Civil War, reproduced it very often, frequently as a "reply" to some other set of verses composed for the occasion, beginning with the words "I ask thee———." A majority of the parodies are based on the converse of the idea which inspired Carew, *e. g.* the poem *On Lesbia*, in MS. Harl. 6918, f. 41, commencing—

"Ask me no more whither doth stray
The sooty night when it is day,
It clothes my Lesbia, dyes her skin
As dark without as she's within."

They are all very poor stuff. The true version was annexed for Pembroke and Rudyard's poems, 1660.

### p. 142. THE SECOND RAPTURE.

This poem was also reprinted in the Pembroke and Rudyard volume, where it is headed *The Epicure's Paradox.*

### p. 151. THE PROTESTATION.

In Add. MS. 11,608, f. 75, is a musical setting of these lines by Nicholas Lanier.

### p. 152. THE TOOTH-ACHE CURED BY A KISS.

In Sloane MS. 1446, f. 61, these lines have the signature "R. Ellice."

ll. 5—10. Cf. Donne, *Anatomy of the World*, l. 91—

"There is no health, physicians say that we
　At best enjoy but a neutrality."

### p. 154. THE DART.

In Sloane MS. 1446, f. 23, these lines have the signature "W. S." (William Strode), and appear among a number of other poems similarly signed.

### p. 155. THE MISTAKE.

In Sloane MS. 1446, f. 87, and in at least two of the Additional MSS. in the British Museum, these lines have the signature "Henry Blunt." They are generally headed in MS. copies, "On a fair lady that wore in her breast a wounded hart carved in a precious stone."

There is a strong likeness to some verses which appear among Aytoun's poems, and also anonymously in several MSS.:

"Thou sent'st to me a heart was crown'd,
　I took it to be thine,
But when I saw it had a wound
　I knew that heart was mine."

### p. 156. ON MISTRESS N.

This poem and the six immediately following were not included in the 1640 edition of Carew's works, and were first added in 1642.

In Addit. MSS. 11,811 and 22,118, where these lines occur, they are headed—"The retired blood exhorted to return in the cheeks of the pale sisters, Mistress Katherine and Mistress Mary Neville."

The two elder daughters of Sir Henry Neville, of Billingbeer (d. 1629), were named Catherine and Mary, and may have been the subjects of Carew's exhortation. Catherine married Sir Thomas Lunsford, and Mary a man of the name of Borell.

## NOTES.

p. 157. UPON A MOLE IN CELIA'S BOSOM.

l. 10. Cf. Donne, Elegy viii. ll. 3, 4—

"As the almighty balm of th' early east,
Such are the sweat drops of my mistress' breast."

p. 158. HYMENEAL SONG.

Lady Anne Wentworth was the third daughter of Thomas, Earl of Cleveland, by his wife Anne, daughter of Sir John Crofts of Saxham. She was born in 1623, and was married July 9, 1638, to John, Lord Lovelace, Baron of Hurley, aged 22. Cf. p. 115.

p. 161. A DIVINE LOVE.

So little of the work of Thomas Carey is known that it would be rash to attribute any poem to his pen on the score of "internal evidence," but if at any time external evidence should be forthcoming that *Divine Love* was written by him, it should find ready credence. The metaphysical vein and the sustained argument are both somewhat uncommon in Thomas Carew, but were probably not so in the author of *Methodus Amandi* (p. 175).

l. 43. *too chaste and fair.* So the edition of 1642, where the poem was first printed. Possibly the right reading is, "Shall she more title gain to chaste and fair."

p. 163. LOVE'S FORCE.

l. 4. *Full-summ'd*, a word (like *imp*, p. 23) borrowed from falconry and used to describe a bird having a complete set of feathers, fully grown. Cf. Milton, *Paradise Regained*, l. 114,

"With prosperous wing full summ'd."

p. 165. TO HIS MISTRESS.

This and the two following poems first appeared among Carew's collected works in the third edition, 1651.

p. 166. IN PRAISE OF HIS MISTRESS.

l. 13. Though "hills of milk" were a favourite subject with most seventeenth century poets, and with none more than Carew himself, there seems to be more than an accidental resemblance between this stanza and another, which occurs in a poem, *On his Mistress*, printed in the so-called works of

Pembroke and Rudyard, 1660, but really written by Dr. William Strode, *To a Lady putting off her veil.*

"Shut from my sight those hills of snow,
Their melting vallies do not show;
Those azure paths lead to despair."

### p. 168. To Celia.

l. 15. *Go I to Holland, France, or farthest Ind.* It is just possible that Carew may have projected a voyage to the Indies. Although he had been to Holland with Sir Dudley Carleton, and to France with Lord Herbert of Cherbury, he may have only mentioned "farthest Ind" in the same connexion for the purpose of asseverating his constancy. But in a letter which Suckling addressed to Carew, he says, "Considering I shall drive that trade thou speakest of to the Indies, and for my beads and rattles have a return of gold and pearl;" and again, "My returns will be quicker than those to the Indies;" it would seem that at any rate Carew had some project connected with the Indies, if not of going thither himself.

### p. 170. To Mistress Katherine Neville.

This poem is not in the editions, but it accompanies the poem on p. 156 in Add. MSS. 11,811 and 22,118, and bears Carew's initials. It is also in MS. Harl. 6918.

### p. 171. Mr. Carew to His Friend.

This poem is not in the editions, but was first printed in Bliss' edition of Wood's *Athenae Oxoniensis* (ii. 659), having been extracted from Ashmole MS. 38, a manuscript which contains a number of Carew's poems, and also certain Psalms purporting to be translated by Carew. It is also found in MSS. Add. 11,811, f. 6, and 22,118, f. 40, in the latter place being subscribed "T. Cary." It is extremely improbable that Carew was the translator of the *Psalms*, and they are not reprinted in this volume. The Psalm (107) chosen by Bliss for reproduction is attributed in Add. MS. 18,220, f. 10, to Lord Digby, Earl of Bristol.

### p. 172. To His Mistress.

This poem was not included in the early editions. It is found in Add. MS. 11,811, f. 6, and bears the signature "T. Cary." It is very much in Carew's manner, and is probably genuine.

### p. 174. On His Mistress Going to Sea.

That this poem and the succeeding one belong to Thomas Carey, son of the Earl of Monmouth, is beyond reasonable doubt. Both appear in *Il Pastor Fido: the Faithful*

*Shepherd, with an addition of divers other poems*, by **Richard Fanshawe, 1648**, accompanied by a Latin translation from the pen of Fanshawe, who attributes the original verses to Mr. **T. C.**, of His Majesty's *Bedchamber*. Both also were reprinted in Henry Lawes' *Ayres and Dialogues*, 1653, and in the table of contents it is expressly stated that the two poems were written by Mr. Thomas Cary, son to the Earl of Monmouth. In the same volume are eight of Carew's poems, and they are put down to him with the description, "Gentleman of the Privy Chamber." Lawes knew both men, and would scarcely have been at the pains of distinguishing their work had one only of them been the author. Neither poem was ever included among Carew's collected poems before Mr. Hazlitt's edition, 1870, but Ellis, in his *Specimens of the Early English Poets*, 1801, printed the *Methodus Amandi* from a MS. lent him by Malone, and assigned it to Carew.

In Sloane MS. **1446**, f. 47, which contains many of Carew's poems, these verses on *His Mistress going to sea* are headed *Mr. Cary of the Bedchamber to Madam Tom*.

### p. 175. METHODUS AMANDI.

This title is that given by Fanshawe to his translation of Carey's *Dialogue* (v. preceding note). There is some uncertainty as to even the poetical name of the lady addressed. Fanshawe called her Eutresia, but in the index the name is changed to Lucretia, and the authorship assigned to "Mistress" Carey. In Ellis' MS. the name is Utrechia, and in MS. Harl. 6917, f. 43, where the poem is subscribed "Sidney Godolphin," it appears as Lucinda.

### p. 179. THE HUE AND CRY.

Although the *Hue and Cry* and the two succeeding poems appeared in the early editions of Carew, it is impossible to ignore Shirley's own claim to them. He published his poems in 1646, and in a postscript gives the following explanation for doing so.

The three poems in question were among those referred to in Shirley's note, and authority of the writer of *The glories of our birth and state*, is, in the absence of other evidence, preferable to that of the "indiscreet collector" who first prepared Carew's poems for publication.

> I had not intention upon the birth of these poems to let them proceed to the public view, forbearing in my own modesty to interpose my fancies when I see the world so plentifully furnished. But when I observed most of those copies corrupted in their transcripts, and the rest floating from me, which were by some indiscreet collector, not acquainted with distributive justice, mingled with other men's (some eminent) conceptions in print, I thought myself concerned to use some vindications and reduce them to my own . . . that other innocent men should not answer for my vanities.

### p. 185. THE GUILTLESS INCONSTANT.

This poem was not claimed from **Carew for** Suckling in any earlier edition of Suckling's work than that of 1696, but it is probable that some good ground existed for the reclamation, as there is no sign of any indiscriminate annexation on the part of the compiler. The most striking evidence in favour of Carew's authorship (beyond its inclusion among his collected works) is in ll. 25, 26, which **are a** variation of Donne's lines in *The Broken Heart*,

"And now, as broken glasses show
 A hundred lesser faces. . . ."

But Suckling **as well as Carew** sometimes helped himself to Donne's ideas.

### p. 191. THE MASQUE.

There is no record of the **circumstances which led to** Carew being selected as Inigo Jones' **collaborator in a** masque, other than is implied in the quotation on the title page that it was by royal command. The year of the performance was 1634, as we now reckon. The entertainment was a **great** success, and awoke the enthusiasm of Herbert, the Master **of the** Revels, who has left on record his impressions.—

"The noblest masque of any time to this day; the best poetry, the best scenes and best habits. The king and queen were very well pleased with my service, and the queen was pleased to tell me before **the king, 'Pour** les habits elle n'avait jamais rien vu de si brave.'"

No doubt the spectacle was a gorgeous one, **but without** the accompaniment of **the** best scenes and the best habits, even the best poetry of this **kind does not** show to advantage. In truth, better masques **than Carew's have** come down to us, but there is many a worse one. **There is** considerable wit and neatness in some of the "topical" allusions, **and the necessary** adulation of Charles and Henrietta is not offensive.

The performance was speedily followed **by** the publication of the text. Perhaps Jones was **responsible for** the insertion of notes like that on p. 227, **on** the reception **of the scenes** and the wonders of the machinery employed, **but the book** was apparently prepared for the press in a hurried **manner.** The masque was reprinted, evidently from the printed copy, **in** the 1640 and subsequent editions of Carew's works, with hardly any alteration, and the same example **has** been followed here, except that the spelling has been modernized. The mis-spelling of some proper names, when it seems **to be** intentional (*e.g.* on p. **197,** "Culabria" for "Calabria"), **has been** retained.

# LIST OF FIRST LINES

|  | PAGE |
|---|---|
| A carver, having loved too long in vain | 146 |
| Admit, thou darling of mine eyes | 153 |
| And here the precious dust is laid | 79 |
| As Celia rested in the shade | 60 |
| As one that strives, being sick, and sick to death | 168 |
| Ask me no more where Jove bestows | 141 |
| Be fixed, you rapid orbs, that bear (*Masque*) | 232 |
| Brave youth, to whom Fate in one hour | 112 |
| Break not the slumbers of the bride | 158 |
| By what power was love confined | 87 |
| Can we not force from widow'd poetry | 100 |
| Cease, thou afflicted soul, to mourn | 88 |
| Come, Celia, fix thine eyes on mine | 50 |
| Dearest, thy tresses are not threads of gold | 136 |
| Fair copy of my Celia's face | 35 |
| Fair Doris, break thy glass, it hath perplex'd | 117 |
| Farewell, fair Saint! may not the sea and wind | 174 |
| Fate's now grown merciful to men | 152 |
| Fear not, dear love, that I'll reveal | 13 |
| Fly not from him whose silent misery | 172 |
| Fond man, that canst believe her blood | 34 |
| Fond man, that hop'st to catch that face | 147 |
| From whence was first this fury hurl'd? | 83 |
| Gaze not on thy beauty's pride | 17 |
| Give Lucinda pearl nor stone | 126 |
| Give me more love, or more disdain | 16 |
| Go, thou gentle whispering wind | 14 |
| Grieve not, my Celia, but with haste | 165 |

## LIST OF FIRST LINES.

|  | PAGE |
|---|---|
| Happy youth! that shall possess | 67 |
| Hark, how my Celia, with the choice | 53 |
| He that loves a rosy cheek | 24 |
| Hear this and tremble all | 115 |
| Hence, vain intruder, haste away | 58 |
| Here are shapes form'd fit for heaven (*Masque*) | 227 |
| How ill doth he deserve a lover's name | 31 |
| I breathe, sweet Ghib, the temperate air of Wrest | 120 |
| I burn, and cruel you in vain... | 46 |
| I heard the virgins sigh, I saw the sleek | 94 |
| I press not to the choir, nor dare I greet | 129 |
| I was foretold your rebel sex... | 22 |
| I will enjoy thee now, my Celia, come | 70 |
| If the quick spirits in your eye | 21 |
| If when the sun at noon displays | 7 |
| I'll gaze no more on that bewitching face | 9 |
| I'll not mis-spend in praise the narrow room | 132 |
| In Celia's face a question did arise | 5 |
| In her fair cheeks two pits do lie | 144 |
| In Love's name you are charged hereby | 179 |
| In Nature's pieces still I see | 6 |
| In the first ruder age, when Love was wild | 163 |
| In what esteem did the gods hold | 85 |
| It hath been said of old, that plays are feasts | 133 |
| Kiss, lovely Celia, and be kind | 149 |
| Know, Celia, since thou art so proud | 23 |
| Ladies, fly from love's soft tale | 19 |
| Lead the black bull to slaughter, with the boar | 108 |
| Let fools great Cupid's yoke disdain | 51 |
| Let him who from his tyrant mistress did | 26 |
| Let pride grow big, my rose, and let the clear | 150 |
| Like to the hand that hath been used to play | 171 |
| Look back, old Janus, and survey | 124 |
| Madam, men say, you keep with drooping eyes | 97 |
| Mark how the bashful morn in vain... | 59 |
| Mark how this polish'd Eastern sheet | 164 |
| Mark how yond eddy steals away | 18 |

|  | PAGE |
|---|---|
| Must she then languish, and we sorrow thus | 42 |
| My first love, whom all beauties did adorn | 185 |
| My Lord, in every trivial work 'tis known | 131 |
| | |
| No more, blind god! for see, my heart | 57 |
| No more shall meads be deck'd with flowers | 151 |
| No, worldling, no, 'tis not thy gold | 142 |
| Now she burns, as well as I | 47 |
| Now that the winter's gone | 1 |
| Now you have freely given me leave to love | 113 |
| | |
| Of what mould did Nature frame me | 143 |
| Oft when I look I may descry | 154 |
| Oh, gentle love, do not forsake the guide | 32 |
| Oh, my dearest, I shall grieve thee | 137 |
| Oh, whither is my fair sun fled | 89 |
| | |
| Raise from these rocky cliffs your heads (*Masque*) | 224 |
| Read in these roses the sad story | 66 |
| Reader, when these dumb stones have told | 81 |
| | |
| Seek not to know my love, for she | 55 |
| Sickness, the minister of Death, doth lay | 48 |
| Sir, ere you pass this threshold, stay | 40 |
| Sir, I arrest you at your country's suit | 109 |
| So grieves the advent'rous merchant, when he knows | 10 |
| Stand still, you floods! do not deface | 140 |
| Stay, coward blood, and do not yield | 156 |
| Stop the chafed boar, or play | 86 |
| Such should this day be, so the sun should hide | 111 |
| | |
| Tell me, Lucretia, since my fate | 175 |
| Tell me, my love, since Hymen tied | 92 |
| That flatt'ring glass, whose smooth face wears | 25 |
| That lovely spot which thou dost see | 157 |
| The harmony of colours, features, face | 78 |
| "The Heir" being born, was in his tender age | 128 |
| The Lady Mary Villiers lies | 76 |
| The purest soul that e'er was sent | 76 |
| Think not 'cause men flattering say | 2 |

|  | PAGE |
|---|---|
| Think not, my Phœbe, 'cause a cloud ... ... | 183 |
| This little vault, this narrow tomb ... ... ... | 77 |
| This mossy bank they press'd. That aged oak ... | 64 |
| This silken wreath, which circles in mine arm ... | 39 |
| Those that can give, open their hands this day ... | 44 |
| Thou great commandress, that dost move ... ... | 125 |
| Though frost and snow lock'd from my eyes ... | 36 |
| Though I must live here, and by force ... ... | 29 |
| 'Tis true, dear Ben, thy just chastizing hand ... | 90 |
| Toss'd in a troubled sea of griefs, I float ... ... | 30 |
| | |
| We read of kings and gods that kindly took ... | 8 |
| Weep not, my dear, for I shall go ... ... ... | 69 |
| Weep not, nor backward turn your eyes ... ... | 68 |
| When I behold, by warrant from thy pen ... ... | 135 |
| When I shall marry, if I do not find ... ... | 160 |
| When in the brazen leaves of Fame ... ... ... | 80 |
| When on fair Celia I did spy ... ... ... ... | 155 |
| When on the altar of my hand ... ... ... | 56 |
| When this fly lived, she used to play ... ... | 52 |
| When thou, poor excommunicate ... ... ... | 20 |
| When you the sunburnt pilgrim see ... ... ... | 33 |
| Wherefore do thy sad numbers flow? ... ... | 63 |
| Whilst thus the darlings of the gods (*Masque*) ... | 230 |
| White Innocence, that now liest spread ... ... | 170 |
| Why dost thou sound, my dear Aurelian ... ... | 104 |
| Why should dull Art, which is wise Nature's ape ... | 161 |
| Wonder not, though I am blind ... ... ... | 45 |
| Would you know what's soft? I dare ... ... | 182 |
| | |
| You that think Love can convey ... ... ... | 54 |
| You that will a wonder know ... ... ... ... | 166 |

---

Richard Clay & Sons, Limited, London & Bungay.

www.ingramcontent.com/pod-product-compliance
Lightning Source LLC
Chambersburg PA
CBHW032044230426
43672CB00009B/1465